FOLK
ART
STYLE

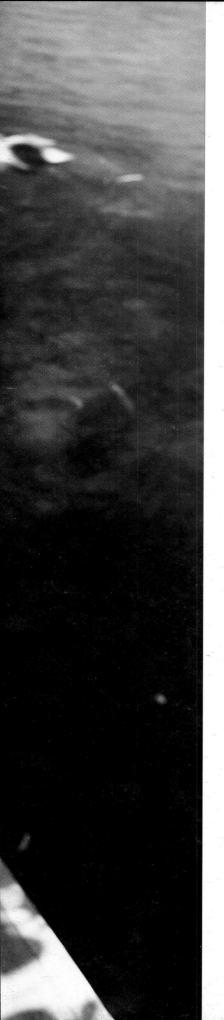

FOLK

TRADITIONAL AND

ART

CONTEMPORARY PAINTING

STYLE

FOR EVERYDAY OBJECTS

SYBIL EDWARDS

Photography by Mark Wood

David & Charles

DEDICATION

*To my sons, Stewart and Andrew, who listen with loving interest
to 'what Mom does'.*

ACKNOWLEDGEMENTS

Thank you, Michael Kay at Tomas Seth for the Jo Sonja paints and sharing ideas about education, Judy Shaw at Trip the Daisy for props and humour, and Jo Curtin for being so marvellously inspiring about the decorative arts generally.

Also, my thanks to Judith Coleridge for the loan of the tray. And remembering why and when it all began, my appreciation and thanks to Bridget Haworth, Lyn Bleiler, Chris Moore and my husband, Mike.

A DAVID & CHARLES BOOK

First published in the UK in 1998

ISBN 0 7153 0688 X

Photography by Mark Wood
Styling by Susan Bull
Book design by Diana Knapp

Printed in Italy by LEGO SpA
for David & Charles
Brunel House   Newton Abbot   Devon

CONTENTS

INTRODUCTION

'The artist isn't a special kind of person, but every man is a special kind of artist.'

A. R. COMARASWAMY

DECORATIVE FOLK PAINTING — THE ART OF APPLYING FIGURATIVE WORK OR DECORATION TO FUNCTIONAL OBJECTS, COMMONLY KNOWN AS 'FOLK ART' — IS AN ACTIVITY WHICH RECOGNIZES THAT EVERYONE HAS LATENT TALENT. WHETHER YOU BELIEVE IT OR NOT, YOU REALLY ARE A SPECIAL KIND OF ARTIST, AND THROUGH THE AGES THE PAINTING STYLES FROM PLACE TO PLACE AND PERSON TO PERSON HAVE BORNE WITNESS TO THIS TRUTH. ARTISTS ARE BORN, NOT MADE, AND THIS BOOK IS FOR EVERYONE.

❧ ❧ ❧ ❧

Folk art has long been associated with a naive, selftaught, folksy approach to the painting of florals, nursery figures and festive themes, which are easily depicted using a specific range of brush strokes. The aim of this book is to push back the boundaries of traditional folk art style to encompass a whole new range of themes and techniques that will appeal to decorative painters of all abilities and tastes. Broadening the language of folk art in this way allows the design and painting of decoration on everyday objects to become as varied and exciting as any fine art pursuit — and the straightforward techniques and stepbystep projects presented in this book will provide the starting point for a fascinating creative journey of your own.

THE ORIGINS OF FOLK ART

People have always applied painted decoration to their surroundings: first in caves, then on handmade implements, then on manufactured goods. The early European folk art traditions began to appear with the rise of the middle classes in the midseventeenth century, for new money could afford to show off the fruits of hard work on modest furnishings in order to mimic the aristocracy and moneyed classes.

Strokework was the common signature of these early painters. Yet, as would be expected, styles were as different from area to area as they were between individual artists. The look of painting on modest objects in middleclass dwellings was described as 'naive' in comparison to the sophisticated decoration applied in grand houses and palaces, and the name 'folk art' was coined by the genteel classes as a way of differentiating themselves from the new merchant class.

Following this great furniturepainting era, which lasted until about 1850, folk art lived on in parts of Europe, but on nothing like the same scale. The surviving practices tended to be quite parochial — traditions were passed down with less of an inclination to experiment. From time to time, however, something unexpected would pop up out of the blue: the relatively recent development of canal boat painting in England is a good example.

In America, the European folk art traditions were adapted and practised by the European settlers, particularly in Pennsylvania, where the German painting tradition that was followed became known as Pennsylvania Dutch (or, more correctly, Deutsch). As time went on, the traditions were passed on and spread to more far-flung regions, but it was all relatively low-key. Toleware – goods made from tin – were the objects most commonly painted.

Like all genres of art through the ages, folk art does not stand still. At times it may lose its popularity, or simply tick over with its pockets of faithful followers, or remain in an indefinite state of inertia, but if any record remains it is always there awaiting rediscovery, revival or adaptation.

THE DECORATIVE PAINTING LEISURE MOVEMENT

In the early 1970s a group of American women, led by Priscilla Hauser and Jo Sonja Jansen, hit upon an idea that would revitalize and popularize 'folk art'. They sensed it could really catch on if promoted properly, and thus the seeds of the decorative painting leisure movement were sown.

This was a startling notion in our stark modern era. Decorative painting was out of fashion, or belonged only to professional bespoke designers and artists. It was time to reclaim and revive the decorative art genre for the ordinary man or woman.

The American 'pioneers' initially borrowed their ideas from Europe. At the formation of the National Society of Tole & Decorative Painters in 1974, the movement could hardly have anticipated the size and scope of its success. Within a year, membership had topped 1,000 and a certification programme was established. The movement gathered momentum, crossing borders and continents.

A few American retail publications began to appear, advocating strokework as the basis of good painting practice. This was supported by the now flourishing teaching studios, which were injecting enormous energy into the move-

ment through their own publications and methods of teaching. Strokework painting now became a unique classification, its principles being used to lead into teaching traditional European folk art styles such as Bauernmalerei, Hinderloopen and Rosemaling. 'Folk art', 'folk painting', 'tole art' and 'tole painting' were the names that seemed to stick in people's minds.

Blended painting techniques, heralded by teachers with fine art backgrounds, also began to be taught as part of the overall discipline, but they usually followed on from basic strokework. Meanwhile, another style had begun to take root in a number of studios. I have called this approach 'bold painting'; its techniques have strong historical precedent, and the style has become extremely popular and is widely practised. These three classifications – strokework, blending and bold painting – are all explored in detail in this book.

DECORATIVE FOLK PAINTING TODAY

With all these new developments now incorporated into decorative painting alongside the traditions of strokework, the label 'folk art' has begun to seem rather too limiting in its scope. The skills and diversity of the art form, not to mention its strong kinship with fine art, dictate the need for a more descriptive label. The status-conscious origins of the term 'folk art' hardly seem applicable in our egalitarian age.

However, to the uninformed 'folk art' continues to convey something of a self-taught, folksy approach. This may have a lot to do with the popular and light-hearted images people like to paint. 'Serious' images and motifs, which have a strong historical precedent across the whole range of decorative art disciplines, are less evident in the folk art repertoire, despite exposure and people's ability to paint them.

For all these reasons, I prefer the term 'decorative folk painting', which encompasses both traditional

strokework folk art and the 'new' techniques of bold painting and blending. As a leisure painting pursuit it is now an established genre worldwide. As a movement, decorative folk painting continues to study in depth, and to forge and maintain links with many world folk painting traditions, especially in Europe. Less conspicuous, however, has been any willingness to address contemporary ideas, particularly those which might appeal to the younger painter with a modern outlook towards art. Perhaps just as fine art rose to new challenges, decorative art will be able to do the same.

The prospects for everyone are exciting, as we deepen our knowledge of past traditions and move into the future with new ideas and outlooks. Members of the global village both contribute to and borrow from each other.

For designers generally, a great challenge lies ahead to develop the field in ever more exciting and diverse ways. There is a wealth of material from which to take inspiration and borrow ideas. There is no need to limit yourself to the folk art traditions — every discipline is at your disposal. But by far the most important source is the creative spirit that lives within us all.

USING THIS BOOK

Decorative folk painting invites everyone to join in the fun of learning to paint. This book shows you the elements and explains the techniques of the three main classifications: strokework, bold painting and blending. You will be able to choose patterns with strokework and blending galore, or something more

restrained from the bold tradition, where design control and clarity come to the fore. If you have a flair for drawing, you will also be able to create your own unique designs using the skills learned here.

The projects that are presented in this book

are deliberately very varied: some focus on traditional strokework; others use the bold painting approach; still others use expressions of the blending technique. The remainder are an integration of all three methods, with perhaps one of them predominating. In this way a huge range of different styles can be achieved, depending upon the balance of the various approaches and the one that you choose to accentuate.

You will also discover that each approach is potentially capable of expressing a wide range of styles: traditional folk motifs, medieval florals, illuminated manuscripts, fine art themes, Art Deco designs, modern minimalism — all these and many more have been used as inspiration for the projects, which demonstrate just how versatile decorative folk painting can be. The traditional rustic look of strokework is easily transformed into Victorian and Edwardian styles, and can even be extended into a form of contemporary expression. Examples of the stylistic versatility of bold painting are thrown up in every age, although it is associated particularly strongly with modern trends. Blended painting can, of course, do anything it wants, but lends itself most readily to trompe l'oeil and classical subjects. By following the detailed instructions and stepbystep artworks, which show exactly how the designs are built up, you will be able to transform readily available, everyday objects into wonderful heirlooms.

Finally, the book covers everything you need to know about preparation and finishing, and about the paints and other products used in this lowcost craft. The shift away from the use of oil paints in favour of acrylics has been very beneficial, their quickdrying properties meaning that a lot of ground can be covered in a relatively short space of time. In addition, there is a range of waterbased mediums which are easily integrated with acrylics and make life much easier all round.

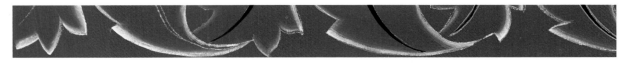

BASIC MATERIALS

DECORATIVE PAINTING NEED NOT BE EXPENSIVE. YOU CAN START PAINTING ON A LOW BUDGET. A FEW PAINTS INCLUDING THE PRIMARY COLOURS, A ROUND BRUSH, A JAR OF WATER, AN OLD PLATE OR LID FROM AN ICE CREAM TUB, PAPER TOWELS, SCRAP PAPER AND MILD SOAP TO WASH OUT YOUR BRUSHES, ARE THE BASIC ESSENTIALS. AFTER A FEW PRACTICE TRIALS, YOU WILL BE CHAMPING AT THE BIT TO TRY YOUR SKILLS ON AN ACTUAL OBJECT. YOU WILL THEN NEED MATERIALS TO ENABLE YOU TO TRANSFER A DESIGN. AS YOUR SKILLS INCREASE, YOU WILL BEGIN TO FEEL THE PULL OF THE FULL RANGE OF EXCITING MATERIALS AVAILABLE TO YOU — AND BEFORE YOU KNOW IT, THERE WON'T EVEN BE ANY RESISTANCE. YOU WILL SOON BE WELCOMING WITH OPEN ARMS AN ARRAY OF NEW PRODUCTS AS THEY HIT THE MARKET.

PAINTS

I prefer acrylic gouache paints to oils because they are enormously versatile. They can be used straight from the tube or bottle, or diluted with water to create subtle washes like watercolour paints; alternatively, they can be mixed with a slow-drying medium to produce the characteristics of oils. Acrylic gouache paints are suitable for most surfaces including wood, tin, ceramics and fabric made from natural fibres.

There are several brands of acrylic gouache paints whose consistency and formulations have been developed especially for decorative painting by drying to a permanent matt finish in comfortable painting time. They are easy to work with and have good coverability. Because they are water soluble when wet, brushes are easily cleaned with mild soap and water.

The recommended brands are Jo Sonja, DecoArt, Delta Ceramcoat, Plaid and Folk Art, but there are others you can use, and there are new brands appearing from time to time too. Acrylic paints without the gouache component can be used but these are not as satisfactory in my view. While some brands don't actually include gouache on the label, the general ambience of the label will help you determine whether they are suitable for the decorative artist.

PAINT COMPATIBILITY

Not surprisingly, mixing paint brands is usually considered inadvisable by the manufacturers! You can often take this with a pinch of salt. However, you absolutely cannot mix water-based paints with oil-based paints in either wet or dry conditions. Until you are thoroughly familiar with the properties of each and learn how to make them compatible (see pages 18–19), it is best to stick to acrylic gouache.

COLOUR CONVERSION CHART

Most decorative paint manufacturers carry large colour ranges, but they don't always use the same names for the same colour. For example, the Jo Sonja colour Norwegian Orange is called Burnt Orange by DecoArt. A colour conversion chart for the major brands is provided on pages 16–17.

BACKGROUND PAINTS

Painting the background on your object uses quite a lot of paint, especially if you are painting something large like a cupboard. Rather than using several small expensive tubes, it's best to use a tin of emulsion (latex) paint or one of Jo Sonja's background paints which come in large screw-lid jars. These are not only less expensive than tubes but they will also accept a large basing brush.

PAINTING EQUIPMENT

BRUSHES

Even your first trials should be attempted with decent brushes to avoid disappointment. Synthetic brushes which are reasonably priced are designed for use with acrylic paints. The lack of standardization in brush sizes between the brands is bewildering, but use the list on page 10 as a general guide. A good brush should not have any stray hairs. A round brush should point well, but you won't know this until you've actually tried using it. On purchase, the brush will be encased in a plastic tube which should be removed and discarded. Although it is tempting to try and replace it, it is not worth it as you risk damaging the hairs. As the hobby takes hold, you can gradually add to your stock of brushes.

BRUSH CARE AND CLEANING EQUIPMENT

If your brushes receive good treatment, they will give you good service for many years. A sound cleaning regime at the end of each painting session is the answer. Stroke the bristles against a mild bar of soap and rinse with lukewarm water, then repeat this procedure until the rinsing water is colourless. Wipe the cleaned brush on a paper towel in the direction of the hairs. Shape the hairs into a nice point or chisel and store upright. If using oil paint, follow the same procedure using thinners or turpentine in place of water.

Starter Brush Kit

- Large (4cm/1½ in) flat brush for base-coating
- No.8 (6mm/¼ in) flat brush or shader
- No.4 round brush (hairs approximately 12mm/½ in long)
- No.1 liner brush (hairs approximately 12mm/½ in long)

PAINT PALETTE

For your initial experiments, use a shallow surface on which to dispense paint, like an old plate, glazed ceramic tile or plastic lid. If you get hooked, I would recommend buying a stay-wet palette. This creates a humid atmosphere around the dispensed paints and prevents the formation of a skin on the surface of the paint. A lid is replaced when you finish painting, and the paints can be reused, sometimes for several days, depending on atmospheric conditions.

BLENDING PALETTE

This is a smooth, flat, non-absorbent surface on which to blend paint into the brush. Find something you can wash off and reuse. If you choose an old

plate, segregate it from your eating and cooking arrangements. I use palette paper which has a waxed surface and comes in a pad. Once a sheet is used up, tear it off the pad and throw it away.

PALETTE KNIFE

You will need an implement for mixing paint, such as a knife or lollipop stick.

JAR

Choose a squat jar rather than a tall one for holding water, because you are less likely to knock it over! Eventually, you may want to replace this with a water basin with a wet compartment in which to rest the brush and a scrubbing compartment in which to clean the brush.

ADDITIONAL EQUIPMENT

PATTERNS

You can draw your own pattern or you can buy pattern books or even single pattern packs.

BLANKS

These are objects with clean unpainted surfaces. Blanks can be wooden, medium density fibreboard (MDF), tin or ceramic.

TRACING PAPER

Use this for copying a pattern and transferring it on to the prepared surface you want to paint.

SOFT PENCIL

A soft pencil will not indent the surface as you transfer the pattern.

GRAPHITE PAPER

Similar in principle to carbon paper, the surface consists of a fine chalk residue which will erase, unlike carbon paper. For more about graphite paper, including how to make your own, see page 25.

COLOURED CHALK PENCILS

These are soft pencils which can be used directly on a surface because they will erase. They are also good for transferring patterns, especially a complicated pattern with lots of lines because the coloured lines allow you to see exactly what you have and have not transferred.

ERASER

This is useful for removing exposed graphite or chalk lines. I use a good-quality putty type, referred to as a 'kneaded' eraser in this book.

BUBBLE PALETTE

A palette with indents is used for additional substances or mediums needed in small quantities.

MASKING TAPE

This is used for holding patterns on to the transfer surface. It is easy to apply and remove.

BROWN PAPER BAG

Used for sanding down acrylic surfaces, this is less harsh than sandpaper.

STYLUS

This is a fine-tipped implement used for making pin-prick dots.

CLEANING SPIRIT

Surgical spirit (rubbing alcohol) or methylated spirit (denatured alcohol) is used to remove minor painting mistakes.

COTTON BUDS

Cotton buds (Q-Tips) are used in conjunction with cleaning spirit to erase painting mistakes.

MASKING FLUID

This is a rubbery solution used to blank out areas you do not want paint to adhere to.

PERMANENT PEN OR BRUSH PEN

These implements are used in place of a liner brush for outlining. For details of using them, see pages 53–54.

TAPE MEASURE

For most purposes, a ruler is used to section off areas on your object for decoration. In the case of round objects, a tape measure fitted around the object provides a good ruling edge.

NEEDLE

This is used for etching or scratching a design into the paint. For best results, this should be done soon after the paint dries and before it cures, which takes approximately 24 hours.

CHISEL

This is used for producing a relief pattern in wood.

ACETATE SHEETS

If you want to test out the viability of a design on an object, paint a rough version on a sheet of clear acetate, then lay it over the object. Using an acetate sheet allows you to make changes to the design.

STRUCTURAL PASTE

This produces a raised design on a smooth surface.

HAIR DRYER

If desired, a hand-held hair dryer can be used to speed up the paint-drying process.

PAINTWORK MEDIUMS

These are mediums used in place of water as the moistening agent as you paint the decoration. For example, if you want to tone down the brush-stroke effect, flow medium can be used. If you want to extend the drying time of the paint to allow more time for blending, you can use slow-drying medium, which is sold under the labels Extender or Retarder. For more about these, see page 32.

ADAPTIVE MEDIUMS

To enable you to use acrylic paints successfully on a range of surfaces, various water-based mediums used in conjunction with the paints allow you to adapt them for painting on a wide variety of surfaces, such as wood, tin, ceramic, glass and natural fibres. All-Purpose Medium can be used on wood and tin, Textile Medium on natural fibres, and Glass and Tile Medium on glass and tiles.

FINISH MEDIUMS

These are water-based substances which can be used in conjunction with acrylic paints to produce a whole range of results and paint finishes, such as a crackled, antiqued or glazed look. These are reviewed in detail on pages 21–22.

VARNISH

If you wish to protect your decoration or create a surface with a certain patina, a variety of water-based varnishes are available, including matt, satin and gloss. They come in liquid or spray form. For details of using varnish, see page 23.

USING COLOUR

Entire books are written on this fascinating subject, but here I only explain a few basic principles so that you can begin painting with a limited expenditure on paints. You will soon realize that using the limited palette is like planting a seed: from three kernels of paint alone — red, yellow and blue — a whole world of colour magic explodes! By adding black and white to the palette, you can then expand the tonal range of each colour, becoming increasingly lighter by adding amounts of white, or darker by adding amounts of black.

❧ ❧ ❧ ❧

BASIC STARTER PIGMENTS

Napthol Red, Ultramarine Blue, Cadmium Yellow, Carbon Black, Warm White (These are all Jo Sonja pigments but you can use appropriate substitutes.)

THE COLOUR WHEEL

PRIMARY COLOURS
These are the colours in the centre of the colour wheel shown opposite. Red, yellow and blue are known as primary colours, which means that they are pure and cannot be reduced or subdivided into anything other than the natural colour they are. The colour wheel demonstrates what happens if you mix two primaries.

SECONDARY COLOURS
These are the colours that appear in the ring around the centre of the colour wheel shown opposite. They are called secondary colours because they result from mixing equal amounts of two primary colours.
Red + Yellow = Orange
Yellow + Blue = Green
Blue + Red = Violet

TERTIARY COLOURS
These colours appear in the outer ring of the colour wheel shown opposite. They are called tertiary colours because they result from mixing equal amounts of secondary colours.
Green + Orange = Olive
Green + Violet = Slate
Violet + Orange = Russet

EARTH COLOURS
In theory, you can go on mixing colours, combining equal amounts of the tertiary colours to get quaternary colours, and so on. However, you may have already noticed in looking at the progressive results that the colours become more sombre and earthy as their brightness subsides. At the tertiary stage, we have come into the earth colour zone. These colours are a strong feature of traditional folk art because earth pigments were always readily available and produced a good background colour for brighter decoration. If you carry on mixing beyond the quaternary stage, however, you eventually come into the mud zone!

You have probably heard the expression: 'the colours were very muddy'. Some artists produce this look by design, but more often they have overworked or overmixed the paint. Undermixing is an easy technique which helps to maintain colour brightness while also achieving a semblance of mixing. (See page 35 for details of undermixing.)

Mixing colours is fun, but it's also a laborious process if you just want to get on and paint. For this reason, manufacturers make life easier by producing a good range of colours which include earth pigments. There are many to choose from but the ones which I would recommend adding to your paint stocks early on are: Payne's Grey, Yellow Oxide, Red Earth and Green Oxide. These colours recur often in the book's projects.

INTERMEDIATE COLOURS
Intermediate colours result from mixing a primary and an adjacent secondary colour. So mixing primary

COLOUR WHEEL

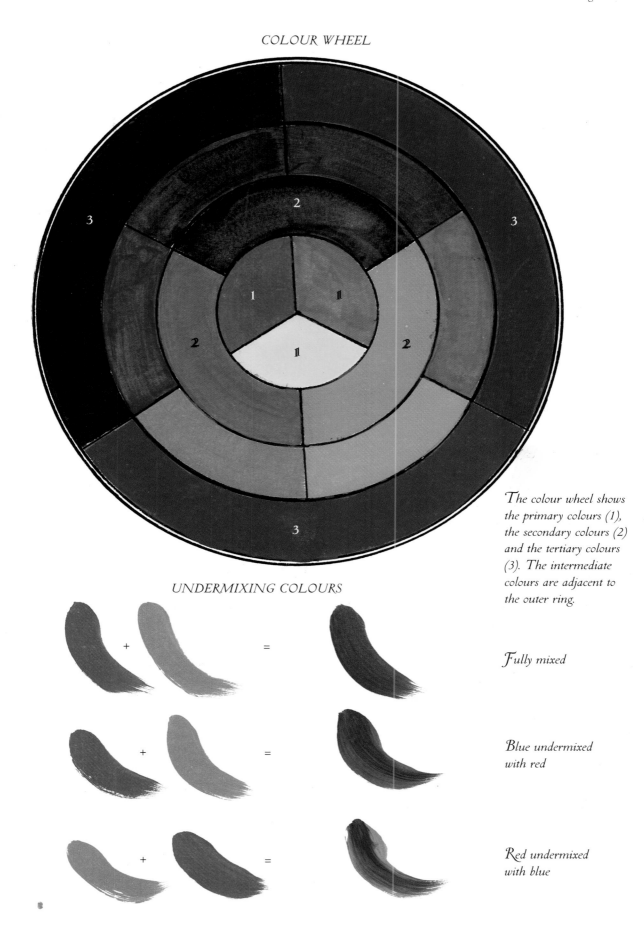

The colour wheel shows the primary colours (1), the secondary colours (2) and the tertiary colours (3). The intermediate colours are adjacent to the outer ring.

UNDERMIXING COLOURS

+   =   *Fully mixed*

+   =   *Blue undermixed with red*

+   =   *Red undermixed with blue*

yellow with secondary orange produces a brighter orange; primary yellow mixed with secondary green produces a brighter green; primary blue mixed with secondary green produces a less bright green; primary blue mixed with secondary violet produces a less bright violet, and so on.

In this intermediate exercise, you may have noticed that some of the results were brighter while others were less bright, and also that one side of the colour wheel is bright, warm and lively while the other side is calm, cool and collected. This gives you some appreciation that colour produces mood as well as sensations of temperature. At the extremes, red is passionate and fiery, while blue is pensive and cool. This information is useful when designing colour schemes of your own.

COMPLEMENTARY COLOURS

Colours that are opposite each other on the colour wheel are called complementary colours. As the name suggests, they bring out the best in each other when standing in close proximity, so a good rule of thumb when trying to decide on a colour scheme is to include these mates! If you actually mix complementaries

together, they have a dampening effect. But sometimes this is beneficial, especially if one or the other colour looks too lively or dominant in your design.

How do you tell if something looks too dominant? If you stand back from your painting and your eye immediately zeros in on one spot from which it can't seem to move, you have probably got a problem. To correct this, tone the dominant colour down with a small amount of its complementary colour.

TONAL SENSE

When you first start to paint, you might be a little cautious and afraid to use colours and their tones effectively. The most common problem is a hesitancy to differentiate tones. For example, let's say the artist has three tones to work with – a light, a medium and a dark. If the tones are strongly differentiated, the effect will be good, even at a distance. If the differentiation is weak, the effect will look rather insipid close-up, and from a distance it won't show up at all. There is little point putting decoration on objects if it fails to make a statement. Understated brashness is better than no statement at all.

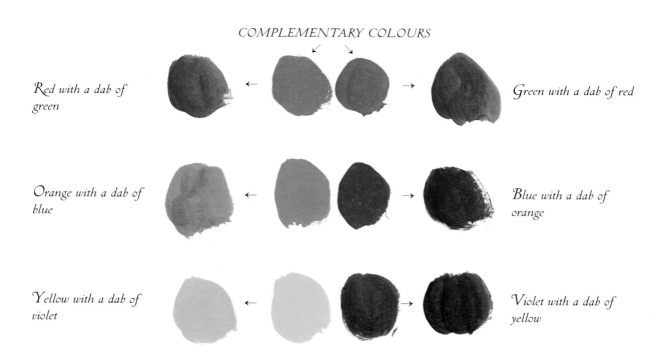

COMPLEMENTARY COLOURS

Red with a dab of green

Green with a dab of red

Orange with a dab of blue

Blue with a dab of orange

Yellow with a dab of violet

Violet with a dab of yellow

GREY VALUE SCALE

Grey contains differing proportions of black and white. Adding grey to any pure colour results in a 'tone'. It ranges in value from dark (1) to medium (2) to light (3).

RED VALUE SCALE

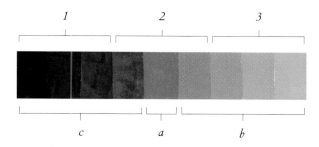

(a) Red – pure colour
(b) Tints of red – adding progressively more white
(c) Shades of red – adding progressively more black
Pure red has a medium value that can be shaded or tinted to dark (1), medium (2) or light (3) values.

COMPARING TONAL VALUES

The leaf painted with 1, 2 and 3 has poor differ-entiation of tone because the tones are too close.

The leaf painted with 1, 4 and 6 has good differ-entiation because the tones are further apart.

OTHER GENERAL RULES TO REMEMBER WHEN PAINTING

Warm colours advance; cool colours recede.

Bright colours advance; dull colours recede.

Light colours advance; dark colours recede.

ACRYLIC COLOUR CONVERSION CHART

JO SONJA'S CHROMA ACRYLICS (CHROMA)	DECOART AMERICANA	DELTA CERAMCOAT	LIQUITEX CONCENTRATED ARTIST COLOURS	FOLKART (PLAID)
Amethyst	Orchid	Lilac Dusk	Parchment + Raspberry + Permanent Light Violet	N/A
Aqua	Desert Turquoise	Laguna Blue	Bright Aqua Green + Navy	N/A
Blue Iridescent	N/A	N/A	Interference Blue	N/A
Brilliant Green	Holly Green	Jubilee Green	Christmas Green	N/A
Brown Earth	Dark Chocolate	Brown Iron Oxide	Burnt Umber + Burnt Sienna	N/A
Burgundy	Cranberry Wine	Black Cherry	Burgundy	Alizarine Crimson
Burnt Sienna	Burnt Sienna	Burnt Sienna	Burnt Sienna	N/A
Burnt Umber	Burnt Umber	Walnut	Burnt Umber + Ivory Black	Raw Umber
Cadmium Scarlet	Cadmium Red	Blaze	Scarlet Red + Cadmium Red Medium Hue	Red Light
Cadmium Yellow Light	Lemon Yellow	Luscious Lemon	Yellow Light Hansa	Yellow Light
Cadmium Yellow Mid	Cadmium Yellow	Bright Yellow	Cadmium Yellow Medium Hue	Yellow Medium
Carbon Black	Ebony (Lamp) Black	Black	Mars Black	Licorice
Cobalt Blue Hue	Ultra Blue Deep	Pthalo Blue	Cobalt Blue Hue	Cobalt Blue
Colony Blue	Desert Turquoise	Avalon Blue	Brilliant Blue + Burnt Umber	N/A
Dioxazine Purple	Dioxazine Purple	Purple	Dioxazine Purple 186	Dioxazine Purple
Fawn	Mink Tan	Bambi Brown	Soft White + Taupe	N/A
French Blue	Navy Blue + Crim Tide	Nightfall Blue	Payne's Grey + Neutral Grey + Ultramarine Blue	Denim Blue
Gold Oxide	Terracotta	Terra Cotta	Raw Sienna + Scarlet Red + Unbleached Titanium	N/A
Green Iridescent	N/A	N/A	Interference Green	N/A
Green Oxide	Mistletoe	Chrome Green Light	Permanent Hookers Green Hue + Baltic Green	Old Ivy
Indian Red Oxide	Rookwood Red	Candy Bar Brown	Burgundy + Burnt Umber	N/A
Jade	Jade + Wedgwood Blue	Leprechaun	Baltic Green + Permanent Hookers Green Hue	N/A
Moss Green	Olive GR + Sable Brown	Olive Yellow	Yellow Oxide + Olive	N/A
Napthol Crimson	Napthol Red	Napthol Red Light	Napthol Crimson	Napthol Crimson
Napthol Red Light	Berry Red	Napthol Crimson	Scarlet Red + Cadmium Red Medium Hue	Christmas Red
Nimbus Grey	Slate Grey + Mink Tan	Cadet Gray	Unbleached Titanium + Neutral Grey	N/A
Norwegian Orange	Georgia Clay	Georgia Clay	Red Oxide + Scarlet Red	N/A
Opal	Warm Neutral Tone	Wild Rice	Parchment + Venetian Rose + Sandalwood	Milkshake
Orange Iridescent	N/A	N/A	Interference Orange	N/A
Pale Gold Metallic	Glorious Gold/M	Gold Gleams	Iridescent Gold	Inca Gold Metallic

JO SONJA'S CHROMA ACRYLICS (CHROMA)	DECOART AMERICANA	DELTA CERAMCOAT	LIQUITEX CONCENTRATED ARTIST COLOURS	FOLKART (PLAID)
Payne's Grey	Uniform Blue	Midnight Blue	Payne's Grey	Payne's Grey
Pearl White	White Pearl	Pearl Finish Gleams	Iridescent White	Pearl White
Pine Green	Avocado	Dark Jungle Green	Yellow Light + Manganese Blue	Southern Pine
Plum Pink	Raspberry	Dusty Mauve	Dark Victorian Rose + Neutral Grey	Raspberry Sherbet
Provincial Beige	Sable Brown	Territorial Beige	Raw Sienna + BAL + Venetian Rose	N/A
Prussian Blue Hue	Midnite Blue	Prussian Blue	Ultramarine Blue + Burnt Umber	Prussian Blue
Pthalo Blue	Ultra Blue Deep	Pthalo Blue	Phthalocyanine Blue	N/A
Pthalo Green	Viridian Green	Pthalo Green	Phthalocyanine Green	Pthalo Green
Raw Sienna	Raw Sienna	Raw Sienna	Brilliant Yellow + Burnt Sienna	English Mustard
Raw Umber	Raw Umber	Walnut	Raw Umber	Raw Umber
Red Earth	Red Iron Oxide	Red Iron Oxide	Red Oxide	Rusty Nail
Red Iridescent	N/A	N/A	Interference Red	N/A
Rich Gold Metallic	Venetian Gold Metallic	Gold/M	N/A	Antique Gold Metallic
Rose Pink	Cad HD + Gooseberry	Crimson + Fiesta Pink	Cadmium Red Medium Hue + Scarlet Red + Sandalwood	N/A
Sapphire	Sapphire	Copen Blue	Ultramarine Blue + French Grey Blue + Phthalocyanine Blue	Paisley Blue
Silver Metallic	Shimmering Silver Metallic	Silver Met. Gleams	Iridescent Silver	Silver Sterling Metallic
Smoked Pearl	Desert Sand	Sandstone	Parchment + Sandalwood	Clay Bisque
Storm Blue	Navy Blue + Black	Dark Night Blue	Navy + Mars Black	N/A
Super Copper Metallic	N/A	N/A	Iridescent Copper	Copper Metallic
Teal Green	Viridian Green	Deep River Green	Real Teal + Phthalocyanine Green	Wintergreen
Titanium White	Snow (Titanium) White	White	Titanium White	Titanium White
Transparent Magenta	Red Violet	Sweetheart Blush	Raspberry	Magenta
Turners Yellow	Antique Gold + Cad Yellow	Empire Gold	Turners Yellow	Harvest Gold
Ultramarine	Ultra Blue Deep	Ultra Blue	Cobalt Blue	Ultramarine
Ultramarine Blue Deep	Ultra Blue Deep	Ultra Blue	Cobalt Blue Hue	Ultramarine Blue
Vermilion	Cadmium Orange	Orange	Scarlet Red + Cadmium Yellow Medium Hue	Red Orange
Violet Iridescent	N/A	N/A	Interference Violet	N/A
Warm White	Buttermilk	Light Ivory	Soft White	Warm White
Yellow Light	Yellow Light	Bright Yellow	Yellow Medium Azo	Yellow Medium
Yellow Oxide	Antique Gold	Antique Gold	Yellow Oxide	Yellow Ochre

PREPARING AND FINISHING

PREPARING AND FINISHING THE SURFACE OF YOUR OBJECT IS PART OF THE PROCESS OF DECORATION. WHETHER YOU ARE AIMING FOR AN ULTRA-SMOOTH SURFACE OR ONE WHICH PRESENTS SOME IMPERFECTIONS, THE MAIN OBJECTIVE OF PREPARATION IS TO ENSURE PAINT ADHERENCE BY CREATING A BARRIER AGAINST ANY VOLATILE SUBSTANCES THAT MIGHT DISTURB THE PAINT SURFACE AT SOME FUTURE DATE, AND TO PROVIDE A GOOD KEY FOR THE PAINT TO ADHERE TO. THIS IS FAIRLY STRAIGHTFORWARD WHEN WORKING WITH 'BLANKS' — UNPAINTED OBJECTS — BUT LESS SO IF WORKING WITH OBJECTS THAT ARE ALREADY PAINTED, WAXED OR OILED.

BLANKS

Blanks are virgin unpainted objects, which can be either bare wood or medium density fibreboard (MDF). In the current market, MDF objects are extremely popular, relatively inexpensive and easily accessible. Most stockists provide excellent mail order services (see Suppliers on page 158).

As a first preparatory step, you may need to fill in the odd gouge or hole in your piece with woodfiller, which is available from any DIY store. When the woodfiller is completely dry, sand it with medium-grade sandpaper, following the grain if the object is wooden. Wipe the surface with a damp cloth to remove the resulting dust.

Now the wood or MDF needs to be sealed with a sealer. This is particularly important on wood which may still be slightly green. If you are painting with acrylics, use a water-based sealer; if you are painting with oils or alkyds, use an oil-based sealer. I tend to use Jo Sonja's All-Purpose Sealer which is a water-based product. All sealers raise the grain of the wood, so after applying it, allow your piece to dry completely, then buff the surface with fine-grade sandpaper or a brown paper bag. Wipe with a damp cloth to remove dust, and your piece is now ready for your imagination.

PAINTED WOOD

REMOVING OLD PAINT

If the paintwork is in a bad state, your piece should be stripped. You can have this done commercially, or you can do it yourself using a proprietary wood stripper, carefully following the manufacturer's instructions. Stripping is best undertaken outdoors or in a well-ventilated room, as the fumes can be quite noxious. You may need several applications. Once all the paint has been removed, rub the piece down with a cloth soaked in white spirit (mineral spirits) to neutralize the effect of the stripper.

RETAINING OLD PAINT

If the paint is in a reasonable condition, you need not apply a sealer. Simply ensure that the paintwork is clean, and then assess whether the old paint is water-based or oil-based before going on to apply your new base coat in your chosen colour. You need to make this assessment in order to determine whether you use an oil- or water-based paint for your new base coat. One way of doing this is to apply a brush-load of water on to the piece.

If the old paint is water-based, the water will adhere smoothly and evenly. In this case you may use

To find out whether the old paint is water-based, apply water. If it adheres evenly, it is water-based.

either a water-based or an oil-based base coat. If you choose a water-based base coat, you may follow with either water-based or oil-based decorative paintwork. If you choose an oil-based base coat, you must follow with oil-based decorative paintwork.

If the original paint is oil-based, the water will not adhere properly and will look patchy. In this case you can only use an oil-based base coat and your decoration must then be oil-based. Alternatively, you can strip off the old oil-based paint as above and then paint with water-based paints.

*H*ere *the original paint was oil-based so the water has created a patchy effect.*

General rule: Oil will cover oil or water, but water will only cover water.

VARNISHED WOOD

If you are painting over varnished wood, you will need to determine first what kind of varnish you are dealing with as both oil- and water-based varnishes are sold nowadays. Follow the above instructions to determine the type of varnish before applying the requisite base coat.

SHELLACKED WOOD

Shellac gives the appearance of varnish but is in fact a spirit-based product and is therefore compatible with both oil-based and water-based paints. In order to distinguish shellac from oil-based varnish, follow the same test as given above.

WAXED OR OILED WOOD

Old wood may have several layers of wax, oil or grease protecting the surface. Use white spirit (mineral spirits) and a pad of fine-grade steel wool to remove these layers. You may need to repeat the process several times. As the wax begins to dissolve, continue rubbing the surface with a soft cloth soaked in white spirit. Then rinse well with water and follow the instructions for painting on bare wood or MDF.

NEW TIN

New tin can be bought with a number of finishes: ready primed but not base-coated, primed and base-coated (black or grey), or unprimed with a shiny metal surface.

Wash unprimed tinware in warm soapy water that is not scented with lemon or lime, as the citric acid in such detergents causes the metal to rust. Rinse well and dry thoroughly using a warm oven or hair dryer. Wash a second time in a 1:1 solution of vinegar and water. Wash again in a non-citric detergent, rinse well and dry thoroughly in an oven preheated to 90 degrees C (200 degrees F), turning it off once the tinware is inserted.

If the surface is shiny, rub very lightly with the finest grade steel wool, taking care not to go through the tin plating. Prime with either a spray or brush-on primer, applying several light coats. Allow each application to dry thoroughly.

Your piece is now ready for sealing. I use Jo Sonja's All-Purpose Sealer which adheres well to tin. Apply the sealer using criss-cross strokes and work in small areas to avoid producing ridges. Continue in this manner, overlapping the sections, until the entire surface is covered. Allow to dry for at least 24 hours.

Finally, apply the base coat as instructed on pages 20–21. If you are using acrylic from a tube which needs thinning, use water-based varnish as a thinner as this promotes better binding. The piece is now ready to decorate. Varnish when completely dry with several coats of water-based varnish or clear acrylic spray (see pages 21–23 for more finishing techniques).

OLD TIN

Rust is the main problem with old tin. Remove it using a wire brush, then sand the surface with fine-grade sandpaper. If there are any scratches, use a pad of fine grade steel wool for final smoothing.

If your piece is heavily rusted you may need to use one of the heavy duty proprietary products available. Other alternatives are sandblasting or having it dipped at a car body shop. This method is recommended for larger objects.

To remove paint, use a commercial paint stripper, following the manufacturer's instructions. Once the paint has been removed, rub the surface down with a cloth soaked in white spirit to neutralize the effect of the stripper. Brush the surface with a commercial rust inhibitor and then proceed as for new tin.

UNGLAZED CERAMICS AND EARTHENWARE

Terracotta tiles and flower pots are easily transformed into decorative pieces by first making sure they are dry and clean, then sealing the pot inside and out using one or two coats of PVA (white) glue diluted with a little water. This will prevent the moisture in the soil destroying the painted surface. Alternatively, use Jo Sonja's Glass and Tile Primer. Then base coat with your chosen colour mixed with Jo Sonja's Glass and Tile Painting Medium. Follow the manufacturer's instructions.

GLAZED TILES, PORCELAIN, STONEWARE AND GLASS

Ceramic studios often sell blanks for decoration, but it can be difficult to key such smooth hard surfaces. Jo Sonja's Glass and Tile Primer, however, has proven very effective. To use this primer, follow the manufacturer's instructions.

Sand the surface lightly with fine grade sandpaper and remove dust with a damp cloth. Apply an even coat of Glass and Tile Primer, brushing it on with a random action to avoid ridges. Dry thoroughly before transferring the design (see page 24). Paint the decoration using Jo Sonja's Glass and Tile Painting Medium in conjunction with the decorative paints, following the instructions.

With porcelain, you may paint directly on to the sanded surface. However, it is advisable to apply a light coating of acrylic matt spray before you begin painting the decoration as this will make it easier to correct any mistakes.

FABRIC

Fabric does not need any preparation, but you do need to choose the right fabric, that is, one that will accept the dye from the painted decoration. Synthetic fibres tend to reject dyes or else the colours do not stay true, so choose natural fibres. Cotton, including canvas, is ideal. The decorative paints need to be combined with Jo Sonja's Textile Medium to convert them for use on textiles. This simple procedure is explained in the manufacturer's instructions.

BASE-COATING

The base coat serves as the background for the decoration and is the surface on which the decoration is applied. You can use either an oil or a water based paint. However, most decorative painters prefer to use an integrated water based system right the way through from preparation to the painted decoration, thus avoiding any concerns about paint compatibility.

PRODUCTS

Paints for base coating and background effects are produced under the Jo Sonja label as background colour paints. The colour range is quite wide, and they are available from art shops. For those working on large items, this has been a very positive development. The background colours come in wide necked jars, so they do not have to be dispensed; a wide base coating brush easily accesses the jar.

Otherwise, you may choose any proprietary emulsion (latex) paint from a DIY store. These paints are water based, and therefore compatible with acrylics.

A third option is to use paint from one of your tubes or bottles. If your piece is quite small, this might be the most cost effective option.

If you want to use oil based paint for base coating, go to a DIY store rather than an art supplier.

TECHNIQUE

A good rule of thumb is to apply several thin coats rather than one or two thick coats as this produces a smoother finish. I find that it usually takes three coats of thin background paint to get a good coverage. To ensure that the paint brushes on freely, dip the brush first in water, then into the paint. The extra water in the brush thins the paint while allowing it to flow more freely with each stroke. Apply the paint in a slip-slap fashion in random directions. This prevents ridging and encourages even paint application. Allow each coat to dry and sand lightly with a brown paper bag before applying the next. Use a hair dryer to speed up drying time.

Base-coating with three thin coats of paint. Each application of the paint is thinned with water to enable easy paint flow which ensures even coverage.

BACKGROUND EFFECTS AND FINISHES

The following decorative effects have all been created with water-based paints, with the exception of the crackle finish and antiquing, which specify other products.

WASHED BASE-COAT EFFECT

Rather than creating a background with one solid colour, you might prefer to use two colours in conjunction to create a more subtle finish. The technique employs three base coat applications and then a fourth application in another colour. This technique was used for the Medieval Floral Screen on page 81.

METHOD
1 Apply three base-coat applications. Allow to dry.
2 Apply one coat of a second colour, working in one direction only. Work with plenty of water in your brush so that the paint flows easily.

GLAZING

This technique differs from the Washed Base-Coat Effect in that the result is more transparent. It was used for the Gustavian Table featured on page 102 and the Elizabeth I Shaker Box on page 86.

METHOD
1 Apply three base-coat applications. Allow to dry.
2 Dispense Jo Sonja's Clear Glazing Medium into a small jar and add a small amount of a second colour. Mix well.
3 Apply this mixture over the surface, brushing out the strokes in one direction to achieve a smooth look. Alternatively, apply the strokes in a slip-slap motion for a rougher look. Allow the paintwork to dry.

CRACKLE FINISH

This technique makes the paintwork crack, giving it an aged look. It was used for the Decorative Landscape Mirror on page 138.

METHOD
1 Apply three base-coat applications. Allow to dry.

A Washed base-coat effect using Cashmere on Azure.
B Glazing effect using Storm Blue over Blossom.
C Crackle finish effect.

2 Apply one coat of Lefranc & Bourgeois Cracking Varnish. Avoid touching it until it is absolutely dry or it will mark.

3 Apply a second coat of Cracking Varnish. Allow to dry. The cracks will not be obvious at this stage.

4 Dab a small piece of sponge into Burnt Umber oil colour, and dab it very lightly over the area of the Cracking Varnish. Avoid using acrylic Burnt Umber as, being water-based, it will lift off the crackle.

5 Douse a soft cloth with surgical spirit (rubbing alcohol) and wipe it over the surface. This cleans off the colour, leaving the contrasting aged cracks.

6 Allow to dry for at least 24 hours, then spray with acrylic satin varnish to seal.

COMBING

This decorative finish was used on the Contemporary Anemones project on page 154.

METHOD

1 Apply three base-coat applications. Allow to dry.

2 Add some contrasting or darker-toned pigment to Jo Sonja's Clear Glazing Medium and mix well. Apply this to the surface to be combed.

D A pattern of ridged lines created by pulling a comb through wet glaze.

E Spirit-rub effect using Burnt Umber over Aqua.

F A lined pattern etched in gold against a black background.

3 While the glaze is still wet, draw a comb over the area to create a straight or wavy pattern. Allow to dry.

SPIRIT RUB

This is a good technique for creating an antiqued look or producing an irregular glazed look in the colour of your choice. It was used on the Charles Rennie Mackintosh Umbrella Stand on page 114.

METHOD

1 Apply three base-coat applications. Allow to dry.

2 Make a watery solution of Burnt Umber. Dip a clean base-coating brush into the solution. Blot out most of the solution on a paper towel. Test the brush on some paper. It should now produce a very light transparent film.

3 Apply this to your object and allow it to dry.

4 Douse a soft cloth with some surgical spirit (rubbing alcohol) or methylated spirit (denatured alcohol) and lightly wipe the surface with it.

ETCHING

Making a fine brocade-looking patternwork against a background is an exciting variation. This technique was used for the Elizabeth I Shaker Box on page 86.

METHOD

1 Apply three coats of Pale Gold to the surface. Allow to dry overnight.

D   E   F

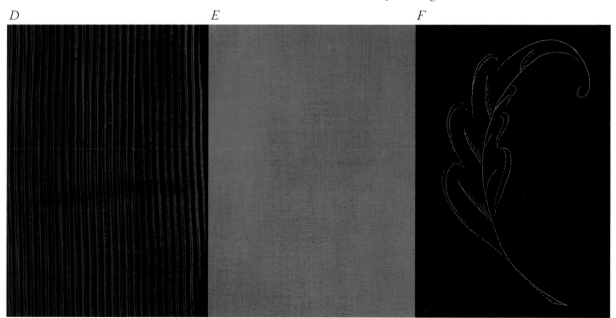

2 Apply two coats of Carbon Black. Leave to dry.
3 As soon as it is dry, transfer the pattern on the surface.
4 Use the end of a compass needle to scratch off the pattern in the paint, following the transferred lines.

The important thing is not to let the second colour harden off. Just after it dries, it is still soft enough to be removed easily with a sharp point.

ANTIQUING

Antiquing is done to give your finished work an aged look. You can antique straight on to your decoration, or over one coat of varnish. Whichever you choose, allow each to dry for 24 hours before antiquing. This was used for the Tray in Pontypool Style on page 110.

METHOD

1 Dab a soft cloth or sponge in a little oil-based Burnt Umber, then wipe it over the surface to be antiqued, building up the look of age in some areas.
2 With a clean soft cloth, wipe the pigment away, leaving some areas looking cleaner than others.
3 Allow the piece to dry, usually for 24 hours, then apply a coat of varnish. Finish the piece with wax to give a more authentic look.

VARNISHING

The durability of acrylic paints means that they will stand up on their own without a coat of varnish but most people feel happier giving their work that extra protection. Varnish can also enhance your work, giving it an all-over consistent finish. Most of the decorative paint brands carry a full range of water-based matt, satin and gloss varnishes. Satin is the safest option, providing a subtle sheen. Matt is a good choice if you want to apply a waxed finish. Gloss is not used so much nowadays because of its high shine, but if you want to impart a period feeling to your work, this is a good choice, as it harks back to the time when gloss was the only finish available.

PREPARATION

Allow your piece to dry for 24 hours before applying any liquid varnish. In the pre-cured state, the decoration is still too tender and might lift off as your wet brush applies the varnish.

Erase any pattern lines. Some can be brushed away with a damp brush while the more stubborn might need further encouragement from a kneaded eraser. Remove any dirt and dust from the piece, to prevent dust particles adhering to the wet varnish.

APPLYING LIQUID VARNISH

Lay the object on newspaper. Stir the varnish gently to discourage too many air bubbles. Using a large base-coating brush, one whose hairs will not drop out, and apply the varnish in a slip-slap fashion, smoothing it out in one direction as you move from section to section. You need to work at a steady pace when using water-based varnish because it dries relatively quickly. For varnishing smaller pieces, this is fine, but for larger pieces of furniture an oil-based varnish might be a more sensible option for the complete beginner. (You can always apply oil-based products over water-based ones, but not vice versa.) As with the base-coating technique, several thin coats of varnish are better than a few thick coats as this gives a much better finish.

Using a brown paper bag, sand lightly between coats when dry, but don't sand the final coat. Two or three coats of varnish are ample.

APPLYING ACRYLIC SPRAY VARNISH

Spray varnish has the advantage over liquid varnish in that it can be applied soon after you finish painting the decoration. Better still, no brushwork is involved so you don't have to worry about the varnish congealing before your eyes because you are not working fast enough.

Prop up your piece on some newspaper. The spray can must be held upright. Spray back and forth across the object in even swathes to avoid spray build-up. If you miss an area on the first go, don't go back. Instead, catch it on the next application. Spray varnish dries quite quickly, so you will be able to add a second and third application soon after the first.

After this explanation you might think spray varnish is far preferable to liquid varnish, so why do I prefer liquid varnish? The reason is that I like to see the artist's hand in the brush strokes as real evidence of a hand-crafted object. However, experiment and use the one you prefer.

PATTERN TRANSFER

The need to work with guidelines or a pattern is a first principle of decorative painting. It ensures that the position of the design on the object you paint does not go askew. The possibility of the design not being straight is increasingly likely if you try to paint directly on to the object freehand. Therefore, even if you pride yourself on being a good artist or designer, it is still advisable to create a pattern unless you are one of the very rare breed with impeccable spatial ability. Many artists like to design and draw their own patterns; others prefer to buy a pattern, or a pattern book, or even a pattern pack which includes colour worksheets along with painting instructions. There is no shortage of choice in this area. (Pattern suppliers are listed on page 158.)

❧ ❧ ❧ ❧

PATTERN APPLICATION

USING SIMPLE GUIDELINES

If your decoration is just a simple design or border, there may be no need to take the trouble of tracing details on to your object. Some simple guidelines will be enough. You can use a chalk pencil to draw them on to your piece in the correct position. For example, a ruled line is all you need for a simple comma border, like the one shown at the bottom of the page.

If you are painting some simple symmetrical florals, use the following guidelines.

Painting around a circle.

Painting around an oval.

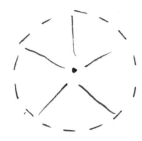  

To paint a five-petalled flower, first sketch the position of the petals, then paint teardrops and dot the centre, or paint flat crescents.

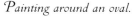

There is no need to trace on commas; simply paint the commas in the measured segments.

USING GRAPHITE PAPER

The simplest and most labour-saving method for pattern transfer is to use graphite paper. It works on the same principle as carbon paper but does not leave indelible lines. Don't be tempted to use carbon paper in place of graphite paper — that is, unless you want black tracing lines in your finished work. A sheet of graphite paper produces fine chalk lines which will erase if necessary.

To use graphite paper, first position your pattern on your piece. Affix it in two or three strategic places with pieces of masking tape. Then place the sheet of graphite paper under your pattern, chalky side down. Now you can begin to trace. When you have finished tracing, remove the graphite paper and the pattern to reveal the transferred design.

Some suppliers sell graphite paper in a range of colours: white, red, blue and yellow. Although it is quite expensive, I recommend having these colours to hand if you do a lot of painting because it means that whatever your background colour, you can select a colour of graphite paper that will either blend in or stand out, depending on your preference for a particular piece.

MAKING YOUR OWN GRAPHITE PAPER

If you are unable to obtain graphite paper, it is quite easy to make your own. Take a chalk stick, place it on its side and rub it back and forth on the rough side of a piece of brown paper. The chalk residue will deposit itself all over the surface of the brown paper. Unlike graphite paper, which uses fixative to make the chalk residue adhere, homemade graphite paper is less sophisticated, but, nevertheless, it does work!

Another way round the problem of having no graphite paper is to take a water-soluble chalk pencil and go over the pattern lines on the back of your pattern, position it on your piece and then trace off.

TRACING PATTERNS

There is no need to trace every little line and detail, just the main outlines. Use a soft pencil and try not to press too hard with it to avoid making dent marks. I like to use a coloured chalk pencil so I can see where I've actually traced. Otherwise it's amazing how you can forget! Some people like to use a fine stylus to go over the lines as this produces crisp fine lines. Remember not to press too hard.

REPAIRING TRANSFERRED PATTERN

Portions of your transferred design might smudge or be erased as you proceed with the painting. You can repair these accidents by replacing the pattern and retracing. A simpler method is to take a chalk pencil and draw in the missing lines freehand.

TRACING PATTERN DETAIL

The initial phase of pattern transfer was simply to transfer the main outline as your guide for the initial stages of painting. When this is completed, you are ready to move on to painting the details. Now is the time to replace the pattern and add the extra detail.

PATTERN ENLARGEMENT OR REDUCTION

The easiest way to enlarge or reduce a pattern is to go along to a commercial photocopying agency where they will do it for you. Nowadays, all photocopiers have this capability. Alternatively, use the pantograph method. Pantographs can be purchased in any drafting or art supply shop. Without access to either a photocopier or a pantograph, the old-fashioned proportional grid method is the ultimate solution! Using a segmented graph, carefully redraw the pattern on a graph that is either larger or smaller, as appropriate, on a segment-by-segment basis.

PLACEMENT OF A DESIGN REPEAT

ALONG A STRAIGHT LINE

Take some brown paper or newspaper and cut a strip the same length as the patterned area you wish to cover. Fold it in half. Fold each half into halves and so on. Unfold the paper and lay it along the length to which the pattern will be applied. With a chalk pencil, make marks on the object to correspond with the folds on the paper. Apply the pattern at each point. This is less awkward than using a ruler, especially if there is a slight curve on the object.

AROUND A CIRCLE OR CYLINDER

If you wish to paint a repeating border design around a flower pot, for example, a chalk pencil is all you need. Place a random chalk mark anywhere on the rim of the pot. Now place another directly opposite.

Do the same to make quarter segments, repeating as necessary.

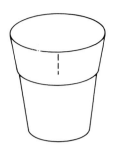 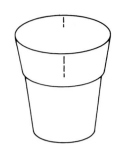

1 Make a random chalk mark on the rim of the pot.

2 Make another mark directly opposite.

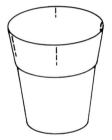 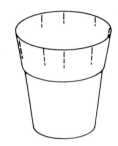

3 Divide into quarters.

4 Repeat as required.

OVER A GIVEN AREA

Cut a sheet of brown paper or newspaper to the size of the area on to which you wish to apply a repeat design. Fold it as shown above as many times as you wish. Then fold it at right angles the other way as many times as you wish. Lay the sheet of paper out flat. Those points where the folds intersect can now be marked with a piece of chalk depending upon how dense you wish to make your pattern. In the example below, alternate intersections are chalked. Press hard with the chalk to leave a good deposit of chalk dust.

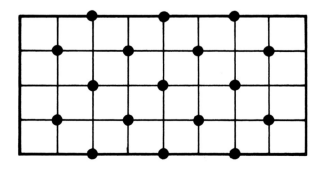

Folded paper with chalk marks at alternate intersections.

Press the chalked side of the paper on to the object, thus leaving behind the chalk deposits as indicators for design repeat placement.

MAKING CORRESPONDING OVAL SHAPES

Quite a number of objects, especially trays, are oval in shape, and it can be a perplexing business making smaller corresponding oval shapes within the overall design. Of course, if you have a very good eye, you will be able to sketch it in, but most of us are not so lucky. Take a ruler and decide your measurement (let's say 5mm/¼in). Butt the end of the ruler against the edge of the tray and make a chalk mark at the 5mm (¼in) reading. Move the ruler along in 5mm–1cm (¼–½in) intervals until you have marked up the circumference of the tray. Join up the chalk marks to form a corresponding oval line.

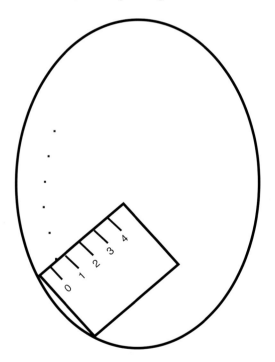

Making a corresponding oval shape.

DESIGN AND COLOUR TRIALS

Deciding colour schemes and/or whether a particular pattern will look good on your object can be quite nerve-racking. What you need is a decision-making aid to get you over these hurdles. A clear sheet of acetate is the answer. Using a non-permanent pen, trace your design on to the acetate sheet, lay it over

Experiment with your traced design on a piece of acetate to ensure a perfect fit on the finished piece.

your object and judge for yourself how it will look or whether it would benefit from a few tweaks. You can also paint your colour scheme on to the sheet and put it to the same test. The pen and paint marks will easily wash off once you have completed your trials.

PAINTING DEAD STRAIGHT LINES

For those of you without a steady hand, use a compass with an ink attachment in conjunction with a ruler with an angled edge. The angled edge is mandatory, otherwise the ink smudges when you lift the ruler. Alternatively, raise the ruler up on to some coins to achieve the same effect as an angled ruler. Permanent ink pens can also be used as a substitute. The ink is permanent when it dries, but until it does dry it will smudge.

CORRECTING ERRORS

If you apply a coat of glaze or varnish on top of your background before resuming the decorative work, this creates a barrier so that the background is less likely to be damaged in the event of having to remove a mistake.

Mistakes can be removed quite easily if the paint has not fully dried. Quickly dip a clean brush in water and brush it over the mistake several times. Tease the stubborn paint away, but avoid being too brutal. You may not be able to remove every last speck of paint or the background paint may look as though it has been affected, but it will be covered by your correction. After 24 hours, you will not be able to remove a mistake with water because the paint will have dried and hardened. However, as a final resort, you may be able to dab it off with a cotton bud (Q-Tip) that has been dipped in surgical or methylated spirit (rubbing or denatured alcohol). Be careful not to drip this over your work as it will leave a mark.

DECORATIVE FOLK PAINTING CLASSIFICATION

THE DIFFERENCES BETWEEN THESE THREE TREATMENTS OF FLOWERS BILLOWING FROM A CONTAINER LIE NOT JUST IN THEIR PATTERNS AND COLOURS, BUT IN THE WAY EACH IS PAINTED. THE PREVAILING TECHNIQUES BEHIND THESE THREE APPROACHES — 'STROKEWORK' FOLK ART, 'BOLD PAINTING' AND 'BLENDING' — ARE EXPLAINED HERE.

❧ ❧ ❧ ❧

STROKEWORK

Below is a very traditional example of strokework painting, or 'folk art'. The whole pattern is created from some basic brush stroke shapes — mainly commas, 'S' strokes and 'C' strokes — which are assembled into the various floral motifs. Oddly enough, even on such a traditional design the overall effect is impressionistic.

There are many traditional European styles of strokework painting — examples include Rosemaling (rose painting) and English Canal Boat — and they are often instantly recognizable. These are the authentic 'folk art' styles, and strokework is the traditional form of decorative folk painting. The strokes themselves limit the possible themes mainly to florals and other natural subjects with flowing lines.

Strokework is often the first port of call for the beginner; establishing good strokework technique is an excellent basis for decorative folk painting of all types, and makes it particularly easy to move into blending. It is also where many a painter remains, for within the traditional strokework disciplines alone there is a great deal to learn and perfect. Some would even say that 'serious' painters begin here — including those who later branch out into fine art disciplines.

STROKEWORK

BOLD PAINTING

BOLD PAINTING

'Bold painting' is the name I use to define a category of decorative folk painting that has been practised widely down the ages and is now becoming increasingly popular, particularly as a starting point for beginners. It emphasizes a limited selection of basic techniques, which at first exclude strokework; these are: basing-in the colours of the main image, lining the based-in areas with a black line, and finally adding some shading and highlighting using the side-loading method. For example, the bright floral cluster below has been based-in with two coats of magenta, lined with black scallops and highlighted with a light tone using sideloading.

The techniques are all easy to learn and the rewards are immediate. Unlike strokework, bold painting allows you to depict a wide range of subjects from the start, from the simple to the sophisticated, traditional to contemporary. For those with an eye for colour, shape and design rather than the brush-handling ability demanded by strokework, bold painting holds a special allure. From this modest beginning, the bold painting school continues to add more techniques, and eventually even strokework may be incorporated.

BLENDING

Although perhaps it shouldn't be, the 'blending' style is regarded by many as representing the equivalent of the 'graduate school' of the decorative folk painting genre. This way of thinking has come about largely because the ability to paint your subjects with greater realism, as an expression of your skills, is perceived by many as the ultimate in artistic progress in decorative folk painting.

Blending incorporates all the techniques used for strokework and bold painting and then adds some more of its own. In the example below, for instance, the florals were based-in with transparent colour using slow-drying medium, which allows more drying time for the paint. The shading and highlights were then blended into this layer while it was still wet. Finally, when these layers were dry, strokework using the sideloading technique and liner work were used to add the finishing touches.

Very often, if the blending style is carried to its extreme the finished result can be quite romantic in flavour. It is therefore important to develop an ability to judge the cut-off point between realism and romanticism – this can therefore become a part of the sensitivity of the blending discipline itself.

BLENDING

VICTORIAN ORNAMENT –
comma strokes

BIRD – adapting stroke-
work to non-floral images

FLORAL GARLAND –
Victorian/Edwardian
Chippendale style

ART NOUVEAU DAISIES –
sinuous liner lines

STROKEWORK PAINTING

These motifs, produced in a range of styles, exemplify strokework technique. The images are mainly floral because they adapt well to the stroke variations. With a little imagination, strokework can also stretch to non-floral ornament.

Simple strokework designs are quickly learned – the tulip border and chrysanthemum sprig are good examples. Loading the brush fully and making the right movement are all that is required. Tipping the fully loaded brush with a second colour in order to produce a variegated effect, and sideloading (a graduated effect) are simple but effective variations of strokework technique.

Strokework has been used through the ages to express nationalistic styles. Rosemaling styles from Scandinavia, for example, feature scroll and line work to produce fanciful florals. Hinderloopen from

GREEK PALMETTE –
classic pattern interpreted
with strokes

CHOCOLATE BOX
HEART DESIGN – very
romantic presentation

DUTCH HINDERLOOPEN
MOTIF – comma scrolls

TULIP BORDER with graduated dots

CHRYSANTHEMUM — basic comma stroke

ROSE — sideloading technique

FRENCH CARTOUCHE — sideloaded roses and grapes

Holland also uses scrolls but the florals are more realistic, combining circles and dipped crescents.

Period effects, whether Art Nouveau, Art Deco, or even contemporary expressiveness, are all within your grasp using strokework technique, as you will discover when you try some of the projects in this book – from the Gustavian Table with Cockerels (page 102) to the Edwardian Tray with Anemones on Stand (page 128).

As you become more proficient you might want to extemporize, as in the example of the floral garland. Departing from perfect stroke shapes to invent some of your own is all part of the fun.

COPY OF DETAIL FROM CHEST from Hallingdal, Telemark, Norway, Bygdoy-Oslo, Norsk Folkmuseum

JAPANESE-STYLE CHRYSANTHEMUM – the commas are exaggerated

CONTEMPORARY DAISY BORDER – basic strokes, jazzy presentation

ART DECO TULIPS – stylized strokework

strokework *techniques*

Similar to learning how to write, strokework entails learning to produce an alphabet of easy brush-stroke shapes. These can then be combined to form various motifs, much as letter combinations form words. The stroke shapes remain a prominent feature of the overall design. Stylistic variations merge as the artist gains the confidence to stray away from rote copybook reproduction.

PAINT CONSISTENCY

ACRYLIC GOUACHE

The more acrylic paints are diluted with water, the more transparent they become, like watercolour paints. This property opens up the field to paint with opaque, semi-opaque/semi-transparent and transparent effects, but in the examples which follow, only the standard effects are shown.

TRADITIONAL MATT STROKEWORK PAINTING

Most strokework calls for a creamy paint consistency to which most brands are formulated. This means that you can load the brush directly from the tube in average atmospheric conditions. If the paint is tacky and will not complete a stroke to your satisfaction, moisten your brush with more water or choose a water substitute.

A runny cream consistency is used for longer strokes and scrolls; a thicker cream-like consistency for short strokes.

WATER SUBSTITUTES (APPLIES TO ALL CLASSIFICATIONS)

Flow medium, clear glazing medium and slow-drying medium can be used as substitutes for water with varying effects.

FLOW MEDIUM helps the paint to flow and is therefore useful for long, unbroken strokes, and also for base-coating small areas which require a smooth finish without brush marks. It dries matt like using water.
CLEAR GLAZING MEDIUM allows you to paint over a larger area before the paint dries; the paint dries transparent with a satin finish retaining the brush marks. It is usually used for backgrounds.
SLOW-DRYING MEDIUM, also known as retarder or extender, facilitates paint flow quite considerably; it ensures plenty of time to make strokes and dries matt. You will need a hair dryer to speed drying time. This medium is also used for antiquing.

This illustration shows how the brush marks are retained without the addition of flow medium.

On the right, clear glazing medium has been used to achieve this satin finish. On the left, slow-drying medium has been used to achieve a more matt effect.

LOADING THE BRUSH

Loading the brush for strokework is not simply a question of dipping it into the paint puddle. That only puts a coating round the hairs. The paint actually has to be drawn up into the hairs so that they hold enough paint to do the job. To do this, first pick up a dab of paint on the brush, then gently press and pull the brush back and forth on the blending palette to encourage the intake of paint at the right consistency to complete the stroke.

FULL LOADING

First moisten the brush with water or medium, then blot the excess water or medium with a paper towel. Pick up a little paint – not too much – on the brush and stroke the brush back and forth on the blending palette until the paint disperses evenly, nearly up to the metal sleeve or ferrule. No blobs of paint should be visible. Repeat the process, taking care not to overload the brush as this will impair performance.

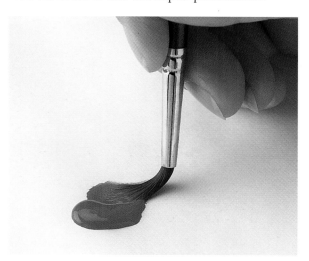

To load fully, pick up some paint from the edge of the paint puddle, then stroke it back and forth to encourage the paint to disperse evenly into the hairs of the brush.

SIDELOADING

Use a flat brush for this process. The effect of sideloading is to create a graduation of colour which fades out to colourlessness. By following an outline with a sideloaded brush, it helps to produce an image with some semblance of form.

For simple sideloading, the paint is pre-mixed to the right consistency so that all you have to do is dip the corner of the brush in it for replenishment. No

blending is necessary. It is a good method if you are doing quite a lot of sideloading in one go. Palette sideloading, on the other hand, is an operation carried out as and when needed in the painting process. It is a slightly more sophisticated method producing an effect that is a little more subtle.

SIMPLE SIDELOADING

Dilute the paint with water or medium in a bubble palette to a runny cream consistency. Moisten the brush, then blot it, broadside, on a paper towel. When the water shine on the exposed side disappears, which will happen almost immediately, dip one corner of the brush into the creamy paint solution. You can now begin to paint.

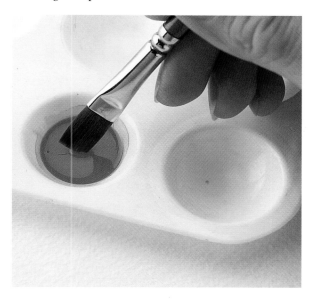

1 Dip one corner of the brush into the creamy solution.

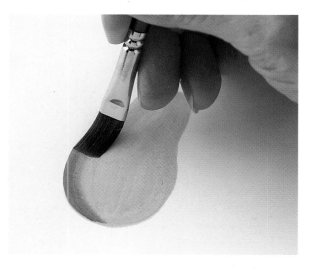

2 Paint around the outline to give the image form.

PALETTE SIDELOADING

This is the standard sideloading method used in the projects in this book.

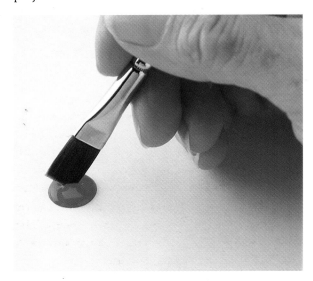

1 Moisten the brush with water or medium as above, then dip a small section of the corner of the brush into the paint puddle. Blot out excess water on a paper towel.

2 Walk it back and forth on the blending palette across a 6–12mm (¼–½in) strip. Now paint your stroke.

SIDELOAD FLOAT

Follow the procedure for palette sideloading, but before you paint your stroke, re-dip the loaded corner section of the brush into water – this will help the paint to flow better. All you want is a tiny amount of extra water with which to lubricate the paint. If you pick up too much water the paint will not adhere cleanly, but will have a runny edge.

After walking the brush on the blending palette, re-dip it into water – just a touch!

DOUBLE LOADING

This type of loading uses two colours which merge in the centre of the stroke. The procedure is the same as for palette sideloading, but has the addition of a second colour on the other corner of the brush to produce a two-toned effect. Walk the brush on the palette until the two colours merge, then you paint the stroke.

Double loading two colours.

LINER LOADING

This method of loading will point up the brush hairs so that you can paint with the very tip of the brush to produce an extremely delicate line. Load the liner following the instructions for full loading (see page 33). If you are painting a very fine line or outline, the brush needs some initial preparation: hold it sideways to the paint puddle and roll it out while pulling with the direction of the hairs.

Hold the brush sideways to the paint puddle and roll it through the puddle.

TIPPING

Use either a round or a flat brush for this process. Fully load the brush with your chosen colour, then dip the tip into a second colour. Now paint your stroke. A variegated, two-tone effect results.

The fully loaded brush is tipped with a second colour.

DRY-BRUSHING

Sometimes you may want a wispy-looking stroke where the paint peters out rather than one of a solid consistency from beginning to end. To achieve this effect, you must either underload the brush in the first place, or load it normally then blot away the excess on a paper towel.

The brush is either underloaded or some of the excess paint is removed.

UNDERMIXING

This is a more sophisticated form of tipping. Once the brush is tipped, it is then rolled out on the palette in the same way as explained for liner loading. This allows more interesting colour variation than with colours that are completely blended.

Undermixing paints creates interesting colour variation, especially when used in leafy strokes.

DOTTING

You can use many implements to create dots, for example the wooden end of your brush, a stylus, or a pencil eraser. You can make a graduated series of dots by repeatedly touching the end of the implement to a surface until the paint runs out.

Dots can be made with the wooden end of your brush, with a stylus or even with the eraser end of a pencil for a more imprecise look.

BASIC STROKE FORMATION

Hold the brush as you would a pen, but more upright. The handle should rest on the middle joint of the forefinger, not in the cradle of the hand. Extend the little finger out for balance and leverage if necessary. Pull the brush hairs behind the handle.

1 The brush is held in a reasonably upright position.

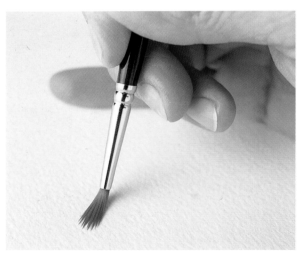

2 The handle pulls the hairs behind it.

COMMA STROKE (ROUND BRUSH)

This is a basic stroke, and created almost as a natural response to the round brush shape as it is pressed on to the surface, drawn along and then released.

1 Hold the brush upright to the surface, using your little finger for balance; you can stretch out your little finger or tuck it under, whichever feels more comfortable.

2 To begin the stroke, gently press the brush on the surface so that the hairs flatten into a rounded shape.

3 Pull the stroke into a gentle curve. The motion is from the shoulder, not the index finger and thumb. Slow down as you make the tail so that the hairs can realign into the natural brush shape. Stop, then lift the brush cleanly off the surface.

CRESCENT STROKE (ROUND BRUSH)

This stroke begins as it ends, on the tip. Control is needed to create the symmetrical shape.

S STROKE (ROUND BRUSH)

To strive towards a perfect 'S' is your goal, but shapes that are somewhat similar are no less appealing.

1 Load the brush fully, so that the bristles come to a point. Hold the brush upright to the surface.

1 Begin lightly skimming the surface using a gentle curving motion.

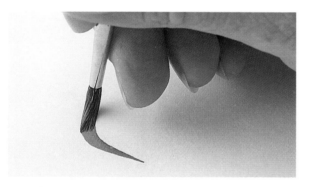

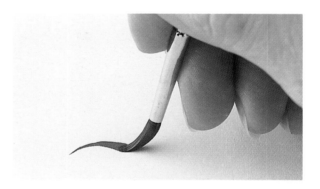

2 Touch the surface with the point of the brush and slowly begin to pull the hairs round while gradually applying pressure. Increase the pressure in the middle section of the stroke.

2 In the middle section, change direction, applying pressure as you do so. When you are beyond the mid-point, begin releasing pressure.

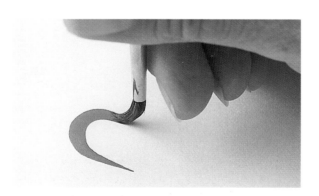

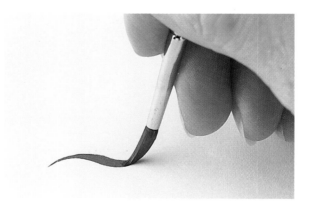

3 Just past the midpoint of the stroke, begin releasing pressure. Slide into the tail. Stop, then lift off cleanly.

3 Nearing the end of the stroke, slow down and allow the brush hairs to realign into a point. Lift off cleanly.

S STROKE (FLAT BRUSH)

The change over from the chisel to the broad side and back to the chisel is easier than it sounds!

CRESCENT STROKE (FLAT/ARCHED BRUSH)

A clean start and finish on the chisel is important. The portion of the stroke created when the brush swings on to the broad side can be a standard crescent or one of the variations shown on page 39.

1 Begin by sliding the brush slowly on the chisel, then as you begin the curve, gradually swing on to the broad side of the brush.

1 Slide for a short way on the chisel, then apply pressure as you move into the curve of the arch. As you sweep on to the broad side the brush will pivot.

2 At the midpoint, exert a bit more pressure. Beyond the midpoint, begin to slow up and release pressure as you change direction, swinging back on to the chisel.

2 Beyond the midpoint, begin to release pressure, allowing the brush to rotate slightly as it reverts back on to the chisel.

3 Finish the stroke upright and cleanly on the chisel. Lift off.

3 With the brush reasonably upright, slide on the chisel. Stop and lift cleanly.

CRESCENT STROKE VARIATIONS

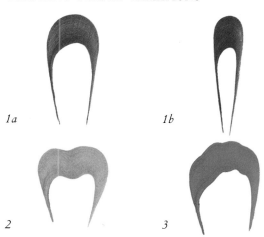

1a *1b*

2 *3*

FLAT COMMA STROKE (FLAT BRUSH)

The flat comma stroke is produced from left to right, beginning at the top of the stroke on the broad side. A number of stroke variations requiring a swivel and pivot motion between the broad side and the chisel are also possible. These flat comma variations are illus-trated on the right.

1 ELONGATED CRESCENTS
The chisel extensions are long in relation to the central broad side section (a). They can also be closer together (b).
2 TOOTH-SHAPED CRESCENT
The brush dips in the central portion of the broad-side.
3 RUFFLED CRESCENT
Unequal pressure from left to right in the broad side section creates a ruffled effect.

1 Begin at the top of the stroke on the broad side, apply-ing even pressure at first.

FLAT COMMA VARIATIONS

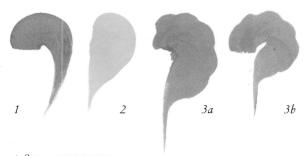

1 *2* *3a* *3b*

1 STRAIGHT PIVOT
The broad side begins on the horizontal and gradually swings then points on the chisel.
2 HEART PIVOT
The broad side begins on the vertical and pivots round in a semi-circle before tailing off into a point.
3 RUFFLED PIVOT
This can begin either horizontally (a) or vertically (b). Uneven pressure creates the ruffles on the broad-side portion of the stroke.
4 LEAF PIVOT
This begins on the horizontal and swivels on to the chisel to make a tail.

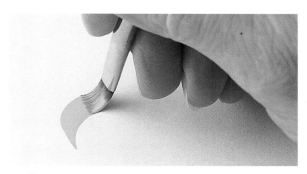

2 Swing on to the chisel into the curve and release the pressure.

4

3 Tail off cleanly on the chisel.

SCROLL STROKE (FLAT BRUSH)

This stroke faces in the opposite direction to a flat comma and is more comfortably produced, beginning on the tail of the stroke and ending on the broad side top portion.

CIRCLE STROKE (FLAT BRUSH)

Circles form the background for many motifs, so it is useful to be able to paint a perfect circle as one stroke. The brush pivots round its axis in a clockwise or anticlockwise direction, depending upon which way you find easier.

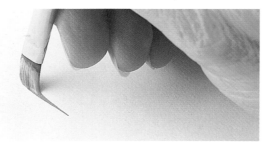

1 Slide the brush a short distance only on the chisel. Then apply gradual pressure, thickening the stroke as it sweeps into a curve. The brush rotates very gradually as it sweeps on to the broad side.

1 Hold the brush upright with your hand and arm angled upwards away from the surface. Bring the chisel down on to the surface with the outside edge at 9 o'clock. Press the brush hairs down flat.

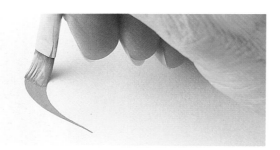

2 Continue on the broad side for a short way, keeping the same pressure.

2 Keeping the hairs flat, begin to twirl the brush by setting up a ratchet motion with your thumb, index finger and middle finger. Sweep the hairs through 360 degrees.

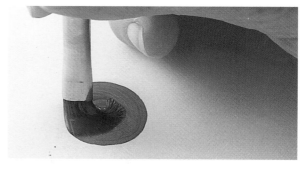

3 Once the stroke is the required length, slow down. Return the brush to the upright position and then lift it off cleanly.

3 Let the hairs fall back into place as you return the brush to 9 o'clock and begin releasing pressure. Lift the brush off cleanly.

Teardrop Stroke (liner brush)

Teardrops can be made by either the sit-down method as shown here or by starting at the rounded portion, similar to making a comma stroke but without the curve.

Scrolls (liner brush)

Scrolls are lengthy, thinner, graceful strokes. Stay loose and free; there is no need to tense just because the strokes are longer.

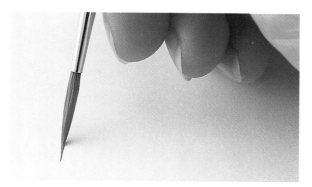

1 Glide down on to the tip of the stroke. Slide the hairs along, applying pressure to thicken out the stroke.

1 Load the brush with paint of a runny cream consistency and hold it upright. Pull the brush along the surface, allowing the hairs to follow the handle.

2 Slow down as you apply more pressure until the brush is sitting on the surface.

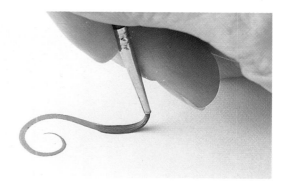

2 As you enter the 'S' curve, apply pressure to thicken up the stroke, contrasting with the thinner sections.

3 Having come to a complete stop, lift the brush away from the surface cleanly.

3 Release the pressure gradually as the curve is completed. Lift off cleanly.

stroke building

A choice of stroke shapes and brush loading techniques enables you to paint a variety of images and patterns as well as to determine style. The following demonstrations consist of basic strokes using round and flat brushes loaded in various ways.

SIMPLE ABSTRACT PATTERNS:
made up of comma strokes alone

1 Precise commas painted with round and flat brushes.

2 Tipped commas created with a round brush.

3 Dry-brushed commas using a flat brush.

4 Undermixed commas achieved with a flat brush.

5 Imprecise under-mixed commas painted with a round brush.

TRADITIONAL FOLK CHRYSANTHEMUM:
precise commas made with a round brush

1 Paint a circle and then the leaves and stem.

2 Add the first pair of outside petals.

3 Paint in the second pair of outside petals.

4 Finally, add the inside petals and paint in dots for the sepals.

LILY:
S, C, and comma strokes with a tipped flat brush

1 Use imprecise flat under-mixed crescents for two petals and a stem.

2 Add the stamen and the first leaf with imprecise flat leaf commas.

3 Paint in finer details lightly with a liner brush and add the second leaf.

4 Finish off the leaves and complete the stamens with light line details.

LILY BORDER MOTIF IN ARTS AND CRAFTS STYLE

LOTUS FLOWER:
William de Morgan style

1 First shape the flower head with undermixed broad strokes.

2 Add broad fillers and use a broad swivel technique for the calyx base and leaf top.

3 Dry brush in the calyx detail and paint a comma leaf.

4 Complete the leaves and details with random undermixed commas.

CHRYSANTHEMUM:
undermixed random shaped flat commas using a dry brush

1 Apply two tone yellow with an oval flat brush for the flowerhead.

2 Add commas in a dark tone for definition.

3 Next, paint in the wing petals of the chrysanthemum.

4 Finally, shape a mixture of leaves and add dots for the sepals.

CONTEMPORARY CHRYSANTHEMUM:
imprecise round undermixed commas

1 Dab in the centre of the chrysanthemum and add the stem.

2 Use tipped regular round commas for the petals.

3 Add medium toned, more irregular commas for deeper coloured petals and a leaf.

4 Complete the flower with darker, irregular commas.

STYLIZED TREES
BALUSTRADE
BORDER

Bird

1 Comma strokes.

2 Graduated commas.

looser strokework

The formal bird pattern above uses loosely packed strokes which work their way around the bird's breast. With experience, you may feel more inclined to suggest the shape of a stroke and to feel your way into a manner of expression which is more personal and/or contemporary in appearance. Stroke suggestion rather than stroke perfection underpins each design in the following examples.

1 Use imprecise commas for the head and wings. Add in the eye and beak with fine lines.

Cherry Blossom

1 Apply haphazard crescents to shape the petals.

2 Continue, varying the colour regimen.

3 Add in the fine line details and dotted sepals.

2 Dry-brush and add tick commas for the wings.

Cherry Blossom Bud

1 Use crescents to suggest the bud shape.

2 Add smaller crescents to provide texture.

3 Complete with small undermixed commas.

3 Complete the wing and tail details with irregular teardrops and add the remaining plumage.

4 Body dash strokes.

3 Vertical dash strokes on wing.

These seagulls can be created using a variety of different brush strokes. Keep your strokes light and allow the brush to run freely to suggest movement.

FUCHSIA

1 First, suggest the dark inner crescents of the flower.

2 Continue to make the flower shape using comma strokes.

3 Add lighter toned commas and complete the details.

CYCLAMEN

1 Shape the flower and leaves with comma strokes.

2 Add a lighter toned comma to the flowerhead and fill in, then dry brush the leaves.

3 Finally, paint in a fine stem and add leaf veins.

SAFFRON

1 Paint in the central teardrop.

2 Add two side teardrops and a stem.

3 To complete, paint the outside petals and leaves.

strokework finesse

Strokes can be used as the building blocks for decoration. You will find that with the support of composition, colour and style, basic strokework becomes an exciting tool for decorative expression. When they are combined with a limited, contemporary colour palette (see below), traditional stroke shapes make a robust statement.

1 Shape the base leaves and flower.

2 Outline with S and C strokes.

3 Finally, add liner and dot details.

BORDER VARIATION

STROKE OUTLINES: SIMILAR TO BOLD PAINTING

mixed stroke shapes can form the basis of effective decoration. This approach helps you to focus on design skills where every stroke counts, rather than excessive or cluttered strokework.

1 Here, the minimalist technique is used to describe a 1970s punk image and is very contemporary in style.

2 The influence of Japanese design in the nineteenth century produced some simple and pleasingly effortless effects.

3 This is Art Deco style. Here, uncluttered strokes in a serialized format produce a feeling of grace and movement.

MONOTONE COLOUR:

The same pattern is used here but this time it is expressed in monotone to produce a less strident design statement. This approach allows you to integrate painted objects easily into almost any room setting.

1   Add the base leaves and flower.

2   Outline with S and C strokes.

3   Complete with liner and dot details.

BORDER VARIATION:

Washed bunches of grapes (Diox Purple) combined with undermixed comma strokes (Jade and Burnt Sienna) are used for the vine leaves. The sideload stroke is created with Pthalo Blue.

UNDERMIXING AND TIPPING:

These techniques allow you to continue to paint without having to studiously load your brush and mix paint. Random, undermixed strokes help to make your design less contrived.

1   Paint the petals with a mixture of Yellow Oxide and Burnt Sienna tipped with Lemon Yellow.

2   Complete the flowerhead and paint in the main lines of the stems.

3   Add dots to the centre of the flower and work the leaves in tipped strokes.

4   Finally, add white dots to the flower centre and fine line details for the leaf veins.

Here, the undermixed and tipping approaches to decoration are brought together in a more stylized pattern.

Although the finished effect looks sophisticated, it is quite simple to recreate.

A simple but
effective cyclamen.

Thistle made from a dry
brushed psychedelic colour.

stroke improvisation

Although perfect strokework is generally taught
as the basis of decorative and folk art, it is also
an extremely versatile 'alphabet' from which a
wide range of styles, including the most contemporary, can be expressed.

Once you have mastered a sound strokework
technique, you can make the transition from
studious strokework shapes to more relaxed ones
to give your work a personal touch. Try to
remember the time when you felt brave enough
to develop your own handwriting shapes and no
longer followed the models in the copybook.
That is what you are being encouraged to do now
– something looser and freer, something that is
uniquely yours!

A daffodil is given a modern,
graphic look.

Subtly apply a tiny
amount of paint and
a slow-drying medi-
um with a flattened
round brush for this
dandelion seedhead.

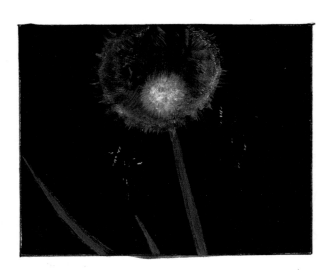

Chrysanthemum
arrangement — loose
leaf with floral
suggestions.

Long, loose shapes dry out
at the end of the strokes for
this tropical plant.

Much of the early folk art strokework, which has become the model for modern decorative and folk art painting, was not as precise as might be imagined. Yet, when developed into a copy-book learning approach, it forms the basis of disciplined and satisfying painting skills which can lead on to a more personal approach.

If you allow yourself to experiment, then you will automatically be preparing for the blending technique which comes later. You might also find that improvisation leads you to invent what you consider to be your own brush-stroke shapes — at least, that is, until you discover them some-where else in the world, as I did on the Indian sub-continent.

This seedhead is
made up of a
limited palette
and brushed dots.

The simple strokes that
make up this iris also allow
the background to work.

BOLD PAINTING

The motifs on these pages use various combinations of the bold painting technique. Subjects can be varied, and designed and painted in an array of styles, while the techniques remain basically the same.

Colours are based in as solid colour, or as a wash or glaze. Whichever method you choose, textures can be superimposed before or even after the base dries. Outlining may be expressed in any colour and using a variety of implements, and can range from thick to thin, sharp to fuzzy. You can also integrate decorative linework, which may be dramatically simple or alternatively quite elaborate. Form may be suggested either by line alone, or with the addition of the side-loading technique.

ANGEL — washing, texturing and lining

DECORATIVE LANDSCAPE — colourful flat glazes

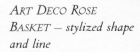

ART DECO ROSE BASKET — stylized shape and line

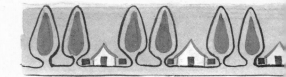

ANTELOPE — *basing, sideloading and lining*

LAMPLIGHTER — *glazing and lining*

ORANGE BUNCH — *decorative line work and sideloading*

DOVES — *shape, colour and line; sideload accent*

At its simplest, bold painting often features great restraint in the painting, to give prominence to a strong design statement. Knowing when to stop painting is as much a part of the decorative creative process as is good painting technique. So, where's the skill? Patience and control are vital, as is a careful use of colour. Sometimes the design comes together only at the lining stage, so have patience. Finally, techniques which might make you wince in the strokework or blending genres are often encouraged here.

FLOWER GIRL — *shape and thick line*

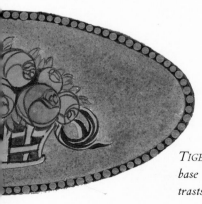

TIGER LILY — *base and wash contrasts; close cropped*

BORDER — *line with a hint of colour*

bold painting *techniques*

The initial emphasis with bold painting is flatness of pattern and structural simplicity. The architect and designer A. W. N. Pugin (1812–1852) was the first modern innovator to acknowledge our medieval heritage in flat pattern and encourage its revival. Basing and lining, which in fine art circles are known as line and wash, are the basis of the technique. Decorative painters have introduced a third technique, sideloading, the effect of which is to produce a naive impression of form on two-dimensional pattern. For this reason, I have coined the name 'bold painting' for the category of decorative painting that uses any combination of these three procedures.

PAINT CONSISTENCY

Bold painting entails basing-in the various elements of the design as the first stage. Most base coats will need two to three applications before complete coverage is achieved.

For most purposes the paint flows and covers with greater ease as a more dilute formula. A higher ratio of water or medium (see page 32) to paint makes for easier painting.

BRUSH LOADING

To save time, work with a fully loaded brush for basing. The lining stage also requires full loading, following the liner loading method (see page 34 for how to do this).

The sideloading stage can use the simple sideloading method, especially if there is a lot to do with one colour. Otherwise, follow the palette sideloading method (see page 34).

BASING

BASING WITH SOLID COLOUR

With most pigments, it takes three applications to achieve an opaque base coat with no brush marks showing through. Of course, you can stop at one or two coats if the effect you are trying to create is less than opaque (for example, a coloured or textured background showing through), or if you want to retain the brush marks. Always allow each coat to dry before applying further coats.

Some pigments, on the other hand, do not cover completely even with three coats – sometimes four or five coats are needed. In the end, it is a question of judgment and personal preference.

As the coats are applied (left to right), notice how the brush marks begin to disappear.

WASHING

By diluting the paint with water to achieve a watery consistency, you can create a transparent wash. While the paint is still wet, the strokes will merge, but once dry, they won't. Of course, this property can be used to your creative advantage, but usually basing entails a merged look. Colour strength will depend on the quantity of pigment used.

Compare the effect of a wash to the based-in example above. The effect is much less heavy.

GLAZING

A glaze produces a similar effect to a wash, using clear glazing medium as a substitute for water. Slow-drying medium will also create a glaze. Clear glazing medium dries with a satin finish relatively quickly although not as quickly as with water. Slow-drying medium dries matt like a water wash, with a slight loss of colour vibrancy, but the slower drying time makes it ideal for coverage of larger areas or for use in hot atmospheric conditions.

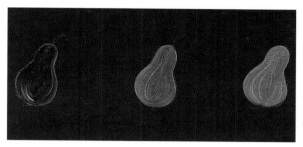

1 Clear glazing medium dries relatively quickly like water but, unlike water, it dries with a satin rather than a matt finish.

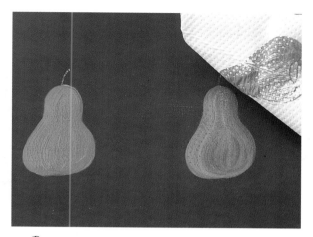

2 Blotting the background with a paper towel before it dries makes for an interesting effect.

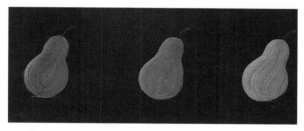

2 Slow-drying medium is very slow to dry. It dries matt like water but with some loss of colour vibrancy.

TEXTURING

Texturing effects can be applied to any based, washed or glazed background once the paint is dry, or even before it dries depending on the effect you want. There are many examples, and, of course, you can invent your own.

LINEWORK

Linework can be used very sparingly, as in the case of simple outlines, or it can be used in profusion as decorative ornamentation. Anything between these two poles, such as shading, is also included.

PERMANENT FELT-TIP PEN OR PEN AND INK

For the beginner, these are the easiest implements to control. A disposable permanent-ink felt-tip pen is the most affordable option. The ink flows in a steady stream and you do not have the nuisance of constantly reloading paint. Ink can be applied very efficiently on top of dry paint, but you cannot vary the thickness of the line as you can with a brush. The look is therefore a bit wooden and naive, but designs can be created to capitalize on this look.

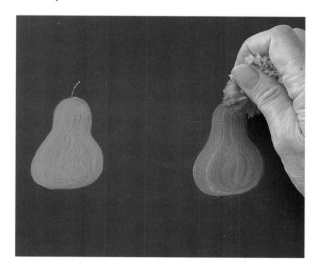

1 Sponging-off some of the paint with a damp sponge before the background dries is an easy variation.

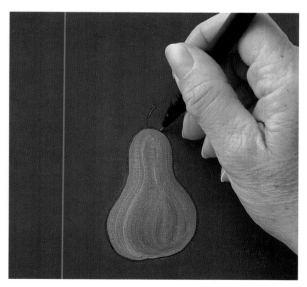

PAINTBRUSH

The liner brush is the implement used by the purist. The artist learns to work with it so that he can produce precise and delicate lines of any width and contour. With practice, you can learn how to load the brush to extend or limit the flow of paint, from a very long scroll to the smallest outline.

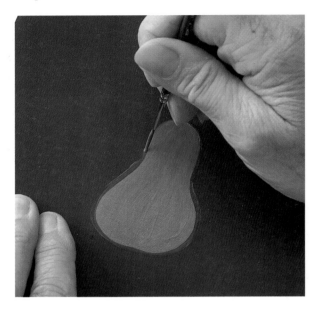

BRUSH PEN

This is a new innovation that is like a cartridge pen except that the nib is replaced by a synthetic brush which is extremely pliable and holds its shape. It produces delicate fine lines as well as thick ones, all without loading and reloading. The brush pen is only available in black. I used it in the Contemporary Anemones project (see page 154).

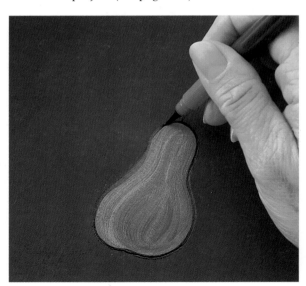

LINEWORK CATEGORIES

Whether you are following the instructions of a pattern or developing your own pattern, you have the artistic licence to use linework in a variety of ways.

THICK OR THIN; ROUGH OR SMOOTH; DIFFERENT COLOURS

The width and fluidity of the outline will define mood. Line texture need not be smooth or flat; it can be rough or raised. You can also vary your choice of colour; it need not always be black.

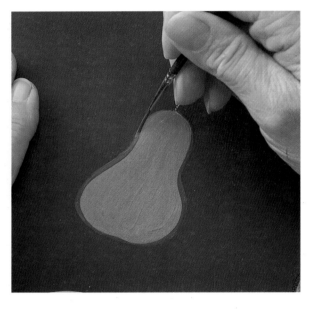

LINEWORK FOR SHADING

Hatching or cross-hatching can be used for shading.

DECORATIVE LINEWORK

You can make linework the main feature of your decorative motifs.

SIDELOADING

Sideloading is a way of altering two-dimensional patterns into the effect of three-dimensional images. While the flatness of pattern is very appealing, a suggestion of form without straying too far into realistic blending can be very interesting and actually quite dramatic.

The various sideloading techniques are reviewed under strokework on pages 33–34.

LINEWORK ORNAMENT

Scrolls, squiggles, curlicues and tendrils are accents often seen in decorative painting. The movement is from the shoulder rather than the wrist, and relaxed.

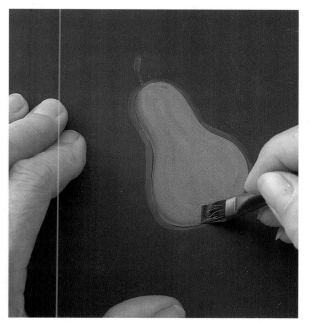

Sideloading is often used in bold painting to alter two-dimensional patterns into three-dimensional images.

bold fruits and flowers

This technique has a more illustrative effect than a painted look and this is mainly due to line definition. The outcome is a clean, lively expression of images. Some strokework resembles bold painting.

APPLE

1 First trace the outline of the apple.

2 Base the apple, leaf and stalk.

3 Outline the apple for definition.

4 Sideload shadows to complete the apple.

PEAR

1 First trace the outline of the pear.

2 Fill in the outline with a wash.

3 Next, add a thickly coloured line.

4 Shade the pear and add dappled dots.

CONTEMPORARY ROSE

1 Trace the outline of the rose.

2 Apply a wash for the leaves and flower.

BORDER WITH MEDITERRANEAN FRUIT AND RIBBON (FROM *PAINT WORKS* BY ALTHEA WILSON)

5 A variation using a wash.

TREE OF LIFE:

The world over, this theme is one of the most popular decorative motifs. To make it look contemporary, I have used bright colours. Follow the same procedure as for the apple, replacing the tracing if necessary for the detail.

5 A bowl of dappled pears.

3 Replace the trace marks and add lining details.

4. Sideload shadows to create depth.

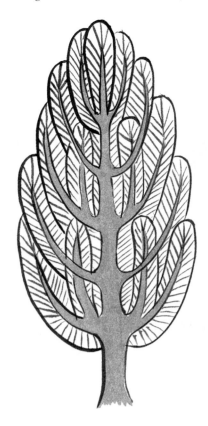

bold painting .... nature

From a stylized tree to an exuberant herbaceous border, this technique lends itself easily to many subjects. It enables a feature to be made of items that might ordinarily be overlooked by the decorative painter – the chestnut leaf, for example. Bold painting sharpens and accentuates details that might otherwise be omitted such as the cut glass Bristol Blue vase motif and it encourages fanciful decorative linework such as the corkscrew flowers and Assyrian tree.

Combine stroke swirls with linework for the tree. Add fine line details for the branches to complete.

1   Apply base.

Exuberant Garden:

Note how the dark tones accentuated with gold produce a sombre, but chic look for this contemporary design.

1 Base each design using a slow-drying medium.

2 The rich, gold lining is serrated with tiny liner ticks. This is a simple, but nevertheless extremely stylish design.

2 Add lined details.

3 Add leaves and colourful flowers in a variety of shapes.

EXUBERANT GARDEN:

Primary colours look very jolly on these simple, floral lined shapes.

1

2

3

bold painting .... figures

Decorative painting can rely almost exclusively on outline. You can be selective here as there is no need to always use all the elements of bold painting together. Observe the René Buthaud design on the right, which emphasizes sideloading. You can also combine line with strokework or simply use line and wash alone.

1   Simple linework and a limited palette makes strong design.

2   The siren is a classical theme expressed in linework and wash. (Designed by William de Morgan.)

3   Graceful lines add fancifulness to these antelopes. (William de Morgan adaptation.)

4   In this Art Deco rendition a sideloaded line replaces a solid one. (René Buthaud design.)

5   Imitation Chinese style using mainly line and wash.

5

4

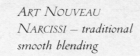

ART NOUVEAU
NARCISSI – *traditional
smooth blending*

GRAPEVINE – *sideloading*

BLENDED PAINTING

Blended painting styles allows you to paint any image, from photographic to impressionistic, with striking realism.

Blended painting is the classification of folk art painting that is most closely associated with fine art technique, but as decorative painters tend to work from patterns and colour sheets rather than from freehand drawings and their own colour sense, they are regarded as a breed apart. Many decorative painters, of course, manage to bridge this gap.

Style variations are open to interpretation, whether expressing period effects, such as the narcissi painted in medieval and Art Nouveau style, or the more classic drapery held in place with a floral ornament.

There are many ways to create the blended effect, the easiest being sideloading and double loading. Another method involves layering transparent coats of different colours. Streak blending, pat blending,

MEDIEVAL NARCISSI –
mop blending

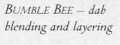

BUMBLE BEE – *dab
blending and layering*

CONTEMPORARY
CINDERELLA'S SHOE –
photographic realism

MAN-IN-THE-MOON —
layering

PEPPERS — contemporary
under-blended look

mop blending and dab blending are other methods of achieving the effect.

The traditional blended look is very smooth and romantic. Brush strokes disappear. Paint is used in a relatively wet consistency and benefits from using slow-drying medium to allow plenty of time to work the paint. A more contemporary look, on the other hand, aims for a rougher texture. The paint is not so wet, giving a dabbed, under-blended impression. Ultimately, you can create whatever style you prefer.

DRAPERY (TOP) — wet blending

PUMPKIN (ABOVE) — layering
and streak blending

MARCH HARE (ABOVE LEFT) —
sideloading, pat blending and
layering

FLEUR-DE-LIS (LEFT) —
sideloading

blending *techniques*

The building blocks of blended painting are *suggested* stroke shapes, in other words they need not be perfect shapes as is the case with traditional stroke-work technique. As you follow contours of the pattern, the shapes you make suggest themselves. The traditional blending technique encourages the shapes to merge and disappear. This is the opposite to strokework painting where the stroke shapes tend to remain visible, often contributing to the overall patterned effect. Contemporary blending styles, on the other hand, are a sort of halfway house. The paint is not heavily worked or blended, nor do the strokes stand alone. If you look at the shoe and the peppers on pages 62–63, you will see the differ-ence between traditional and contemporary blending.

Blending can be a surface process, a depth process or a combination of the two. With the former, the merg-ing of strokes across the surface is what blends the colours together. With the latter, it is the build-up of paint, layer upon layer, which creates the translucent colour shimmer.

PAINT CONSISTENCY

TRADITIONAL BLENDING

A slightly wetter paint consistency makes for easier blending, as does diluting paint with the slightly oily slow-drying medium rather than water. This medium allows a smooth flow of paint over quite a large dis-tance or for a considerably longer time. As the brush depletes, even a small amount of medium enables painting to continue. This means that you can work with the paint quite thinly, thus accentuating its transparent properties.

By comparison, diluting paint with water speeds up the drying time but it dries more opaque. Your choice will depend on the effect you are striving for and the ease with which you can use water instead of slow-drying medium.

CONTEMPORARY BLENDING

A rougher, less finished look is often associated with the contemporary look, so working with paint that is tacky or thick is an advantage in achieving this effect, especially when you come to the overpainting stage – that is, painting on to the base paint. Discovering methods which will encourage the paint to go on in a more pasty manner in short strokes is all part of the fun.

Blending the paint on the palette until it 'begins to bite' is a method I use before actually applying the paint. I used this technique for the painting of peppers which is shown on the previous page.

1 Stabbing the palette over and over with a flattened loaded brush encourages the paint to go tacky.

2 The tackiness of the paint helps to produce the desired pasty effect.

Brush Loading

Full Loading

Full loading is illustrated on page 33. The brush is fully loaded when building up layers of paint, especially if you are covering a relatively large area. Use slow-drying medium if you want to accentuate a lighter, more transparent look.

Flat Loading

Applying very thin applications of paint is more easily controlled when painting with a flattened round brush. The rounded end is nicely contoured to conform to most pattern shapes and you can work with a very light touch. Dampen the brush hairs, flatten them out between your thumb and forefinger, then pull the brush through the paint and slide off in the direction of the hairs.

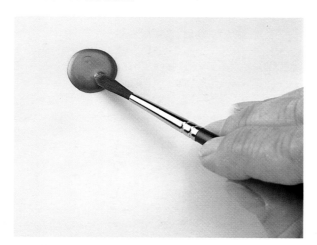

1 Touch the hairs on to the edge of the paint puddle.

2 Blend the paint on the blending palette, moving with the direction of the hairs.

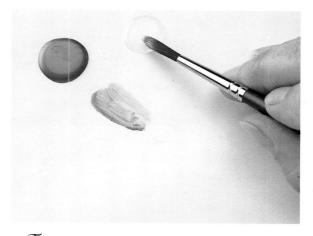

3 Touch the hairs in a tiny amount of slow-drying medium in order to discourage the brush from drying out too quickly.

Coating

With experience, you will notice some pigments, such as white, seem to lose their punch if applied with a fully loaded brush. The trick in this case is to load the brush partially and then dab it once more into the same paint, but do not blend it into the brush. Let it sit on the outside of the hairs as a coating, then begin to paint. This is a useful technique for the more contemporary look.

1 Partially load the brush.

2 Tip the partially loaded brush with the same colour.

SURFACE BLENDING TECHNIQUES

SIDELOADING

Sideloading has already been covered under Strokework (see page 33) and Bold Painting (see page 55), but it is also included in the battery of techniques for Blending. Indeed, it is the most basic of the blending techniques and is especially useful for small or tight areas that need shading and highlighting, such as grapes. On larger areas, sideloading is a good technique by which to achieve the heavily romanticized look we associate with much decorative folk painting (see page 70).

Sideloading is a quick way of shading and highlighting small areas; otherwise brush blending is more convenient.

BRUSH BLENDING

Repeated stroking with the brush, and teasing out the paint in the direction you want it to go, is a way of achieving a smooth transition from one colour to another. A more streaky effect might be your aim as

1 Repeated stroking while releasing pressure as you walk the brush sideways blends one colour into the other.

2 A few light finger dabs or mop pats help to blend the paint at the point where it begins to trail off.

opposed to one where the brush strokes completely disappear. If you cannot get a smooth transition with the brush alone, do not hesitate to use your finger or a mop brush. A few light pats just where the strokes trail off or appear to merge is all that is needed.

Combining the paint with slow-drying medium allows you extra time to play with it. You only need a tiny amount of medium in order to promote better lubrication.

MOP BLENDING

Use a fully loaded round brush and dilute the paint with slow-drying medium rather than water. Apply the paint mixture into the centre of the general area where you wish to apply a shadow or highlight. Now use the mop to tease out the paint until it fades away into nothingness.

1 Dab some paint mixture on to the surface.

2 Tease the paint out from the centre so that it fades gradually away.

Combining the paint with slow-drying medium gives you more time to engage in the teasing-out process. If you are working on a small area, using the medium will not be necessary, but on larger areas it is absolutely vital.

Pat Blending

Use a flattened round brush to apply the paint. As it is applied, tease it out in the same way as mop blending to produce a lightly textured effect as you pat (see Queen Elizabeth's hair on page 90).

Pat blending with a flattened round brush builds an interesting texture as it fades away.

Dab Blending

This is a technique I recommend for the contemporary look. The brush has been partially loaded and coated using the same colour for each, then repeatedly stabbed on to the palette to encourage the paint to become tacky. Instead of making proper strokes with gentle beginnings and endings, the paint is dabbed on in short circular movements to encourage a pasty rather than smooth look.

Short pasty strokes are the effect of dab blending.

Dry-brushing, Blushing and Dusting

These are words used to express degrees of subtlety for dry-brushing (see page 35). Dry-brushing is relatively coarse and achieved with a standard round brush; blushing is relatively fine-textured dry-brushing with most of the applied paint removed either by mop or by finger; while dusting is just the merest hint of dry-brushing created by a gentle sweeping across the surface.

Depth Blending

Layering

This entails the application of two or more transparent coats of paint. They can all cover the same area or simply overlap in selected places (see page 52).

Sinking Colour

If a coloured or shaded area is too prominent, it can be sunk into the paintwork by adding a layer of transparent paint (see Georgia O'Keefe Revelry project on page 142).

1 The lines look very prominent painted on to the background.

2 Under one layer of paint wash the lines are less prominent, and they recede even more under a second layer.

simple blending

The blending technique helps to build form into images but also (particularly in the case of contemporary styles) makes them exciting by exploiting a textured, rather than a smooth effect. Romantic technique aims for a dreamlike smoothness of form whereas the classical approach is for natural realism. Use a slow-drying medium to replace water as a thinner. (A hair dryer speeds up the drying process.) The technique of simple blending (illustrated on this page) combines basing and side-loading to create blended integration of strokework with background colour; use a slow-drying medium and a mop to soften out the pigment.

BELL FLOWER

1 Base the petals.

2 Apply a darker shade.

3 Next, sideload the central stroke.

4 Finally, sideload commas.

LEAF

1 Apply the base.

2 Add a darker shade.

3 Sideload the leaf shape.

4 Line for definition.

ROSE

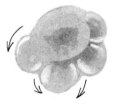

1 Apply and then darken the base.

2 Next, sideload the outer petal strokes.

3 Sideload the bowl shapes.

4 Add sideload strokes inside the rose.

With two colours (Warm White and Burnt Sienna), a tremendously interesting yet subtle design is created using the simple blending method of light onto dark.

double loading

The colour blend created on the brush is transferred to the painted surface. (See page 34 for the double loading technique.)

ROSE:
placement of double-loaded rose pink and smoked pearl petals round a circle

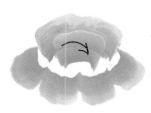

1 Paint four outer petals.

2 Add a large humped crescent above them.

3 Paint a smaller crescent slightly lower than the first.

4 Add another (concave) crescent above the petals.

5 Add an S stroke on the right.

6 Fill the gap with a shallow left comma.

7 Add the finishing stroke.

LEAF:
double loaded Teal Green and Jade

1 Pull and pivot your brush with a wiggle movement.

2 Repeat on the other side.

3 Add the veins with fine line details.

Make sure that the lighter colour is kept on the outside of your brush strokes. Placing the petals in the right position is half the battle. You can always add some more petals at different angles in the gap between the main bowl and the outer petals.

the romantic look

This popular style creates a dreamlike quality with all the irregularities and blemishes completely smoothed out. You will find that the mop brush is a good aid for this look. (See page 66.)

PLUM

1   Base the plum in a light tone and the leaf in a medium tone.

2   Shade the edge of the plum with a medium tone and highlight the leaf in a light tone.

3   Mop the edges of the leaf, highlight and add more shading.

4   Shade the outside of the plum with a dark tone; also the central leaf.

5   Mop shade on the leaf and glaze the plum with Burgundy.

6   Add the leaf veins and stem. Highlight and shadow the plum.

DEWDROP

1   Base the dewdrop shape.

2   Add the highlights.

3   Finally introduce shade.

A favourite ploy of those who follow the romantic look is to add a dewdrop. This puts the final touch to the image of perfection.

classical expression

A natural look is the aim of this school. Blemishes are retained and there is less attempt to arrange the components of the image in a favourable position. Layering of paint is often employed. (See page 67.)

PLUM

1   Base the plum, twig and leaf.

2   Add a darker tone to the plum and blot it. Sideload the leaf vein.

3   Sideload light highlights and add a dark tone for the leaf glaze.

4   Blot the leaf glaze and add a dark tone plum glaze.

5   Line the leaf and add some light plum highlights.

6   Shade the leaf, twig and plum stem.

Here, the strokes are blended but this is a more realistic example which includes the blemishes and natural features. The colours are also natural. All this is achieved in the same number of steps as the romantic version opposite.

contemporary approaches

The accentuation of texture and the bold use of colour are the province of contemporary design. In terms of texture, it is the reverse of the romantic style but, like romanticism, it has its own exaggerative quirks and these are often in the form of colour.

RED PEPPER:
Use dab blending for shading and highlighting

1   Base with Napthol Red Light and then retrace the design.

2   Apply dry pigment with irregular light dabs.

3   Dab white highlight over the surface.

4   Shade the dabs to make the pepper stem.

AUBERGINE (EGGPLANT)

1   Apply a light base with DA Dusty Rose.

2   Blot the base with Red Violet glaze.

3   Continue to blot with Payne's Grey glaze.

4   Complete with some dabbed highlights.

I chose bright green to complement both the pepper and aubergine (egg-plant). The effect is very lively because these are complementary colours (see page 14).

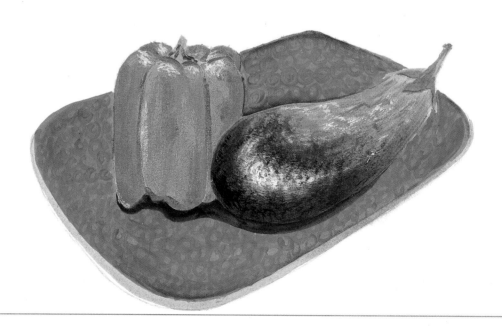

decorative finishes

Some of these techniques are very effective for creating textured designs. Here, I abandon the paintbrush for part of the job and use the simple blotting method using a paper towel. The image is distorted in order to accentuate the contemporary look.

URN

1 First, apply blotted Bronze glaze.

2 Next, add blotted Magenta glaze.

3 Continue with blotted Pthalo Blue glaze.

4 Finally, mop out the Pthalo Blue glaze.

LEMON

Here three yellow tones (light, medium and dark pigments) are applied with thick dabs.

1 Base of medium tone.
2 Dabbed dark tone.
3 Dabbed light tone.
4 Details in Moss Green.

1

2

3

4

The completed composition of the distorted vase with lemons scattered against a blue and white checked background produces a contemporary mood.

THE PROJECTS

THE FOLLOWING STEP-BY-STEP PROJECTS PUT INTO PRACTICE ALL THE DECORATIVE FOLK PAINTING TECHNIQUES DESCRIBED IN THE FIRST SECTION OF THE BOOK. EACH PIECE IS PAINTED IN A PARTICULAR STYLE: THIS COULD BE STROKEWORK, BOLD PAINTING, OR BLENDED PAINTING — OR IT MIGHT INTEGRATE ALL THREE IN ONE PROJECT. YOU WILL DISCOVER THAT THE SOURCES FOR INSPIRATION ARE SO DIVERSE, FROM KNOWN PAINTING STYLES TO SOURCES YET TO BE EXPLORED, THAT THE RANGE OF PAINTING POSSIBILITIES SEEMS ENDLESS.

❧ ❧ ❧ ❧

PROJECT NOTES

Before you try the projects, read the following notes which apply to all the projects in the book.

❧ Water-based rather than oil-based products have been used for each project, and the actual materials you will need are specified. However you don't have to keep to these specifications. If you have oil-based paints by all means use them, but be sure to remember the rules of paint compatibility (see pages 18–19). If you are going to buy paints acrylic gouache (see below) are my recommendation as they are easy to use and dry relatively quickly.

❧ A number of manufacturers produce integrated ranges of products for the decorative art market. I have used Jo Sonja's Artist's Colours (acrylic gouache) almost exclusively for all the projects in this book, with the occasional use of DecoArt (identified as DA before the colour). I have also used mediums and background paints from the Jo Sonja paint range. If you are using another manufacturer's pigments, refer to the colour conversion chart on pages 16–17 to help you select your colours. Suppliers are also listed on page 158.

❧ You will find a wide selection of blanks available for painting and decorating. They can be readily obtained from the suppliers and mail order companies listed on page 158, and decorative art painting studios also tend to carry a good range of products.

❧ Where mixes of paints are recommended, the proportions are approximate.

❧ Brush sizes are given for each project — substitute a similar size from your own collection if you do not have the exact size to hand.

❧ The patterns may be enlarged or reduced as appropriate (see page 25).

PAINTING TIPS

❧ When painting large areas such as backgrounds or sub-backgrounds (see Cachepot project on page 106), work with quite a lot of water in your brush to encourage the paint to spread quickly and evenly. This will prevent the paint from becoming gummy and creating ridges.

❧ If you want a particular area of your painting to have the strongest colour clarity possible, underpaint the area with white.

❧ Always keep a colour-free, wet brush available. If you make a mistake or paint over a line, you can then quickly brush it off before it dries.

❧ Preparing the palette versus brush mixing: I find the former a waste of paint, so I do all my mixing by brush in small amounts as I go along. You may find that the paint dries up too quickly in which case substitute slow-drying medium for water.

❧ If you don't have all the recommended colours for a project don't worry — you can substitute colours quite successfully and perhaps make a few discoveries for yourself.

❧ When mixing paint always add darker colours last. This avoids wasting paint.

❧ Strokework technique versus blending: with the former, the brush is fully loaded, but with the latter, it's best to work with small amounts of paint in the brush together with slow-drying medium.

❧ If you are worried about smudging completed areas, place a sheet of acetate over the work for your hand to rest on.

❧ If you wish to make contact with teaching studios, you should ring or write to your national society of decorative painting (see page 158) who keep a record of all affiliated teachers.

MEDIEVAL ILLUMINATED HATBOX

ILLUMINATED MANUSCRIPTS ARE A WONDERFUL SOURCE OF RICH, DAZZLING MATERIAL. MUCH LIKE DECORATIVE PAINTERS, ILLUMINATORS OFTEN WORKED FROM PATTERN BOOKS AND AS DEMAND FOR THE WRITTEN WORD INCREASED, SO THE PATTERNS WERE TRACED RATHER THAN COPIED TO SPEED UP THE OPERATION. IN MANY CASES, STEP-BY-STEP PAINTING INSTRUCTIONS WERE ALSO PROVIDED. THIS STRONGLY COLOURED DESIGN IS BASED ON A CUTTING OF A FIFTEENTH-CENTURY DECORATED INITIAL EXTRACTED FROM AN ITALIAN CHORAL BOOK. I LOVE ITS SCROLLWORK AND FANCIFUL MEDIEVAL FLORALS, WHILE THE OVERALL SHAPE MAKES THE DESIGN PERFECT FOR A CIRCULAR HATBOX. THE ORIGINAL IS PRESERVED IN THE VICTORIA & ALBERT MUSEUM, LONDON, ENGLAND.

Painting Style

This is mainly a bold-painting project. Some blending is required on the flower petals, calyces and tendrils, while the scrollwork around the edges employs the sideloading technique. Using retarder (slow-drying medium) rather than water to thin the paint allows it to run smoothly over the relatively long areas of application

• m a t e r i a l s •

❧ *HATBOX, APPROXIMATELY 45cm (18in) IN DIAMETER*

❧ **BASE COAT**
Cobalt Blue

❧ **FINISH**
Water-based varnish

❧ **PALETTE**
Cobalt Blue, Pale Gold, Carbon Black, Warm White, Cadmium Scarlet, Cadmium Yellow Mid, Jade, Brilliant Green, Burnt Sienna

❧ **BRUSHES**
6mm (¼ in) flat, 12mm (½ in) flat, No.4 round, No.8 round, liner

❧ **OTHER SUPPLIES**
Fine-grained sandpaper, brown paper bag, tracing paper, graphite paper, chalk pencil, masking tape, soft lead pencil, stylus, slow-drying medium

BASE COAT

1   Sand the box with fine-grained sandpaper.
2   Base coat the lid and sides with three coats of Cobalt Blue, allowing to dry after each coat and then sanding lightly with a brown paper bag before applying the next coat.
3   Paint the inside of the box in the same way with Cobalt Blue or any preferred colour.
4   Transfer the outlines representing the thick black borders on to the box lid (see page 24).
5   Next, base in the centre portion with three coats of Pale Gold.
6   Finally, base in the thick border lines with Carbon Black.

WHITE SCROLL SECTIONS

1   Transfer the pattern into each section.
2   Add a tiny amount of Warm White to some slow-drying medium. Base in the areas as indicated in the right-hand section on the illustration opposite, using a No. 8 round brush. Allow to dry.
3   Using a 12mm (½ in) flat brush, highlight the areas as shown with sideloaded Warm White.

4   Add the faint squiggle detail with a liner.
5   Add the dots with a stylus.
6   Line the motifs with Carbon Black as indicated in the left-hand section.
7   Use a stylus to apply the dot crescents with Warm White.

CENTRAL CAMEO

For the correct painting order, follow through quadrants 1–4, which illustrate how the design builds up. Apply the instructions for each quadrant to the whole motif.

COLOUR KEY

1 *Cobalt Blue*	5 *Brilliant Green*
2 *Cadmium Scarlet*	6 *Carbon Black*
3 *Cadmium Yellow Mid*	7 *Warm White*
4 *Jade*	8 *Pale Gold*

QUADRANT 1

1   Transfer the pattern outlines only.

2   Load a No.8 round brush with Cadmium Yellow Mid and base in the exotic flower centres.

3   Base in the flower petals, alternating Cobalt Blue and Cadmium Scarlet as shown.

4   Using a No.4 round brush, base in the Cobalt Blue and Cadmium Scarlet leaf sections.

5   Base in the leaves and tendrils with Brilliant Green and Jade mixed 1:1.

6   Reapply the pattern and transfer the detail on the central flower segments.

QUADRANT 2

1   Using a 6mm (¼in) flat brush, outline the pattern detail on each central flower segment with sideloaded Burnt Sienna.

2   Flatten the hairs of a No.4 round brush and use it to mix a tiny amount of Warm White retarder. Lighten the petal and leaf areas as shown.

QUADRANT 3

1   Using a liner, first outline the petals with Warm White.

2   Add the Carbon Black stripe to each petal.

3   Use a stylus to add the graduated dots with Warm White.

QUADRANT 4

1   Flatten the hairs of a No.4 round brush and paint highlights on to the calyx, leaves and tendrils in Cadmium Yellow Mid.

2   Using a liner, add the Carbon Black outlines.

BOX SIDE (ACANTHUS MOTIF)

1   Transfer the pattern (see page 24) omitting the yellow stripe.

2   Outline the acanthus chain with sideloaded Warm White using 12mm (½in) flat brush. Wet the brush with slow-drying medium rather than water to aid the paint flow over such long stretches.

3   Add the Carbon Black vein.

4   Outline the black vein with Warm White.

5   Now, reapply the pattern and transfer the remaining stripe.

6   Outline the acanthus chain with Carbon Black.

7   Finally, lightly brush in the stripe with Medium Cadmium.

MEDIEVAL FLORAL SCREEN

Floral sprigs were a common feature of tapestry, embroidery and illuminated manuscripts during the Middle Ages. They were usually decoratively arranged on slender stems to show off full blooms, buds and leaves, rather than as they would appear in nature. Shadows were also introduced as a design feature to accentuate these elements. Following in the medieval tradition, the designs in this project are set against a gold background to striking effect.

Painting Style

This is primarily a bold-painting project. The various elements are based-in, then shades and highlights are created by the sideloading method. Stems and leaves consist of undermixed green and burnt sienna tones and their details are applied with a liner

• m a t e r i a l s •

❧ *FOUR-PANELLED GOTHIC SCREEN*

❧ BASE COAT
Deep Plum, Dolphin (Jo Sonja's background colours or similar substitutes)

❧ FINISH
Permanent pen, acrylic spray, water-based varnish

❧ PALETTE
Pale Gold, Rich Gold, Cobalt Blue, Payne's Grey, Warm White, Cadmium

Yellow, Pine Green, Moss Green, Green Oxide, Burnt Sienna, Cadmium Scarlet, Napthol Red Light, DA Baby Blue, Teal Green, Colony Blue, Cadmium Yellow Light, Fawn

❧ BRUSHES
Large brush, 2.5cm (1in) flat, liner, No.4 round, 6mm (¼in) flat, No.3 round

❧ OTHER SUPPLIES
Brown paper bag, tracing paper, graphite paper, chalk pencil, ruler, stylus

BASE COAT

1   Scale up the pattern (see page 25) to fit the size of your screen.

2   Using a large brush, apply two coats of Deep Plum background colour to both sides of each panel of the screen, sanding each coat with a brown paper bag when dry.

3   Overpaint the panel fronts with one coat of thinned Dolphin background colour. Brush on the colour lightly so that the Deep Plum shows through. Allow to dry.

4   Lay the scaled up diamond pattern on top of each panel front in turn and transfer the outside lines (see page 24) using a ruler to ensure you achieve straight edges.

5   Mix equal amounts of Pale Gold and Rich Gold and base in the diamonds with two or three coats using the 2.5cm (1in) flat brush.

COLOUR KEY	
1 Cobalt Blue	9 Cadmium Scarlet
2 Pale Gold	10 Napthol Red Light
3 Rich Gold	11 Pine Green
4 Warm White	12 Green Oxide
5 Payne's Grey	13 Moss Green
6 Cadmium Yellow Light	14 DA Baby Blue
7 Cadmium Yellow	15 Colony Blue
8 Teal Green	16 Fawn
	17 Burnt Sienna

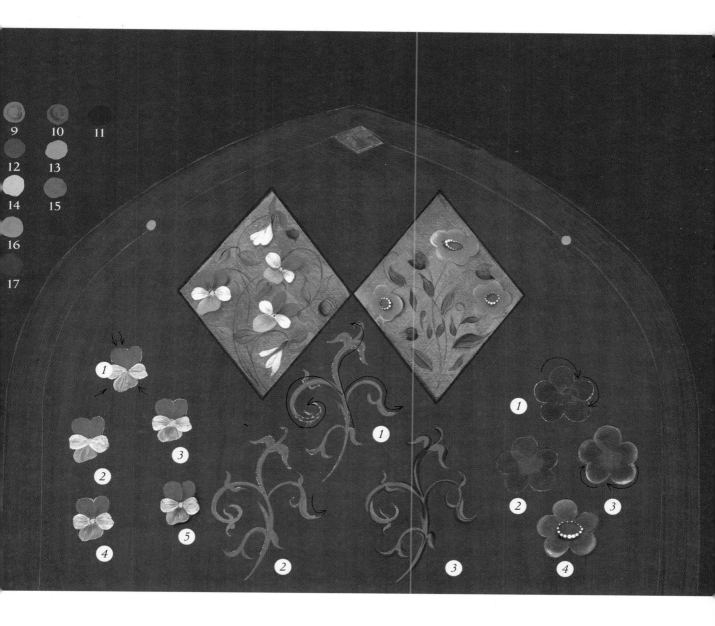

6 Position the floral patterns with leaf ornaments on each facing screen. Place one leaf ornament facing left, the other right. Transfer in place.

BLUEBELLS

1 Using the No.4 round brush loaded with Cobalt Blue, paint the central teardrop, followed by comma strokes on either side.

2 Using the 6mm (¼ in) flat brush, apply a sideload of Payne's Grey in the 'V' as illustrated.

3 With the same brush, apply a sideload highlight in Warm White.

4 Dot in the Cadmium Yellow stamen. Apply the leaves using undermixed Pine Green and Moss Green, and the stems using undermixed Green Oxide and burnt Sienna. Add sideloaded Payne's Grey shadows as illustrated.

STRAWBERRIES

BERRY

1 Base in the berries with Cadmium Scarlet using the No.4 round brush.

2 Sideload the right-hand shadow with Napthol Red Light and a touch of Payne's Grey.

3 Apply the left-hand highlight with a sideload of Warm White.

4 Use undermixed greens as above for the leaves.

5 Load the liner tip with Payne's Grey and touch-brush the small seeds.

BLOSSOM

1 Paint the petals using a flat crescent stroke in Warm White.

2 Flatten the No.3 round brush and add the centre in Cadmium Yellow.

3 Sideload DA Baby Blue and apply it to the edge of each petal.

4 Apply a very light sideload of Teal Green around the yellow centre.

5 With a Payne's Grey sideload, apply petal shadows as illustrated. Shade the bottom portion of the yellow centre.

LEAVES

1 Base the leaves with two undermixed green strokes using the No.4 brush.

2 Apply dark veins with a liner.

3 Using the same brush, outline the jagged edge with Payne's Grey.

VIOLETS

1 Using a No.3 round brush, paint the petals in this order: Colony Blue, Cadmium Yellow, Warm White.

2 Dab the centre with Cadmium Yellow Light.

3 With a liner and Payne's Grey, apply the radial lines from the centre outwards.

4 Go around the centre with a broken line of Payne's Grey.

5 Shade round the blue petal and around the bottom of the white petals with a sideload of Payne's Grey.

6 Add the leaves and stems following the previous instructions.

PERIWINKLE

1 Base the petals with flat C strokes using a 6mm (¼ in) flat brush loaded with Cadmium Scarlet.

2 Paint the centre with Napthol Red Light.

3 Go around the petals with a 6mm (¼ in) flat brush sideloaded with Warm White.

4 Using a stylus, apply dots around the centre in Warm White.

5 Add shading with a sideload of Payne's Grey.

6 Apply leaves and stems as before.

7 Add shading around the blooms and some of the leaves with a sideload of Payne's Grey.

ORNAMENTAL SPRIGS

1 Using a liner loaded with Colony Blue, paint the main central stem first. Then add the limbs.

2 Add the Fawn extensions.

3 Add Payne's Grey shading using liner strokes.

FINISHING

1 Use a permanent pen and ruler to outline all the diamonds.

2 Allow to dry for 24 hours, then apply a coat of acrylic spray over the area containing the floral diamonds to fix the ink from the permanent pen. Then apply two or three coats of water-based varnish, allowing each coat to dry before applying the next. Sand lightly between coats with a brown paper bag.

ELIZABETH I SHAKER BOX

ELIZABETHAN PORTRAITURE IN THE SIXTEENTH CENTURY HAD MANY PARALLELS WITH DECORATIVE PAINTING. ONCE THE FIRST PORTRAIT WAS PRODUCED, REPRODUCTIONS WERE MADE FROM IT ON A COMMERCIAL SCALE. STUDIOS WERE EQUIPPED WITH A PATTERN TAKEN FROM THE ORIGINAL. THE OUTLINES WERE TRANSFERRED EITHER BY TRACING OR BY PRICKING HOLES THROUGH THE PATTERN, THROUGH WHICH CHARCOAL DUST WAS SHAKEN. THE OUTLINES WERE FILLED IN WITH REFERENCE TO INSTRUCTIONS ON THE PATTERN. THIS WAS THE MEDIEVAL EQUIVALENT TO THE MODERN PROCESS OF PRODUCING PHOTOGRAPHIC ICONS. HUNDREDS – AND SOMETIMES THOUSANDS – OF COPIES WERE MADE TO SATISFY DEMAND!

● m a t e r i a l s ●

⟩ SHAKER BOX, *36cm × 25.5cm (14½ in × 10½ in)*

BASE COAT
Cobalt Blue, Pale Gold

FINISH
Water-based varnish

PALETTE
Cobalt Blue, Pale Gold, Carbon Black, Colony Blue, Rich Gold, Burgundy, Vermilion, Burnt Sienna, Yellow Oxide, DA Slate Grey, Warm White, DA Flesh

Tone, DA Sable Brown, DA Shading Flesh, Jade

⟩ **BRUSHES**
Large brush, brush pen, 12mm (½ in) flat, No.4 round, liner, No.2 mop, 3mm (⅛ in) flat, No.3 round, No.8 round, 6mm (¼ in) flat

⟩ **OTHER SUPPLIES**
Brown paper bag, clear glazing medium, tracing paper, graphite paper, chalk pencil, large sharp needle, slow-drying medium, stylus, Burnt Umber artist's oil colour, soft cloth

Painting Style

● *This project uses all the techniques of folk art. The detail is the main emphasis. Sleeves, lace ruff, jewels and an etched brocade background comprise an exciting challenge* ●

BASE COAT

1 Using a large brush, apply two or three coats of Cobalt Blue over the box base and lid, sanding between coats with a brown paper bag when dry. Leave to dry.

2 Mix Pale Gold with clear glazing medium. Glaze the box base and lid lightly with a large brush, applying the strokes horizontally across the surface. When dry, trace on the Armada pattern (see page 24).

3 Fill in the pattern using a brush pen.

MAIN PATTERN

Centre the pattern on the box lid and transfer the main outlines only (see page 24). The illustration shows the procedure for basing on the left side of the illustration. Addition of detail is shown on the right side of the illustration.

BROCADE WALL BACKGROUND, DRAPERY AND BOX BORDER

1 Using a 12mm (½in) flat brush, apply two or three coats of Pale Gold first, then two coats of Carbon Black, allowing to dry between coats. Trace on the detail of the brocade pattern. Using a large sharp needle, scratch off the black paint along the traced lines to reveal the gold underneath. This procedure must be done as soon as the black coat is dry, before the paint hardens off.

2 Using a 6mm (¼in) brush, paint highlights with a sideload of Colony Blue. Add the drapery border and fringe with Rich Gold.

3 Trace the box border on the box. Paint it as shown with Carbon Black using a liner.

CHAIR AND TABLE

Use a No.4 round brush for all instructions except where otherwise indicated.

1 Make a mixture of slow-drying medium and Burgundy. Base-in the chair and table, applying just enough to allow the blue background to show through. Apply more paint on the folds of the tablecloth. Allow to dry.

2 Pat Vermilion along the folds and on the table top to suggest the texture of velvet.

3 Load a liner with Rich Gold and paint the tablecloth fringe as illustrated.

4 Paint the chair knobs first with Burnt Sienna and then highlight with a sideload of Yellow Oxide.

DRESS BODICE AND SKIRT

Use a No.4 round brush for basing.

1 Base-in the dress with two coats of Carbon Black. Trace on the main central design. Paint in the outlines with Rich Gold as illustrated at the bottom of the skirt. If you mix the paint with plenty of slow-drying medium and roll it out, you can paint almost continuously.

2 Dot in all the pearls with DA Slate Grey. Using a stylus, highlight with dots of Warm White. Paint in the gems: Burgundy with a touch of Warm White, and Cobalt Blue. Paint the gold casements in Rich Gold highlighted with Pale Gold. Highlight the gems with a dot of Warm White.

3 Trace on the pearl necklaces and chatelaine. Follow the instructions above for painting the pearls, gems and gold.

SLEEVE

1 Using a No.4 round brush, base-in the sleeve with two coats of DA Flesh Tone, and allow to dry. Then base-in with Warm White and leave to dry. Trace on the pattern.

2 Paint the black detail with a liner, then follow the instructions above for the gems.

3 To apply shadows on to the puffs along the sleeve edge and the elbow creases, sideload with DA Slate Grey and shade.

4 To paint the cuffs, follow the pattern for painting the ruff.

HAIR AND RUFF

1 Using a No.4 round brush, base-in the face and ruff with two coats of DA Flesh Tone mixture; base-in the hair with Vermilion mixture.

2 Paint the ruff pleats with a sideload of Warm White. Outline the points of each pleat with six scallops, paint the two parallel lines across the pleat, adding the vertical line detail, the criss-crosses, the wheel, and finally the line and dot. Use a concentrated mixture of Warm White and slow-drying medium. Roll the brush through it into a nice point, then paint on the very tip.

3 Dab Burgundy mixture along bottom of ruff (2) then soften it out with finger or a mop (3). Repeat along the top of the ruff.

4 Trace on the sheer outer collar. Outline with Rich Gold. Shade along the inside of the outline with a sideload of Carbon Black.

5 Flatten a No.4 round brush, pick up a small amount of Warm White mixture and paint wavy hair highlights. Begin very lightly dabbing from the forehead, then twist the brush more on its side as you move towards the back of the head (3). Blend Burgundy mixture into the hair on the left-hand side to shade.

6 Trace on the jewels and paint them following the previous instructions.

FACE AND HANDS

1 Trace the features. Shade the side of the face and forehead, eyebrows, nose and chin with a side-load of DA Sable Brown (2). Accentuate the eyebrows and eye features with a liner. Paint the whites of the eyes with Warm White mixture, then blot. Repeat with more Warm White to build up the whiteness. Paint the lips with DA Shading Flesh. Blot and repeat (3).

2 Dab Warm White mixture on to the face (3), softening it out with a mop. Repeat two or three times to build up the facial highlights. Dab DA Shading Flesh on the cheek areas, softening it in with a mop. Paint the centre of the eyes. Dab and repeat. Darken the lips slightly with Burgundy, then dab.

3 Outline the fingers with Burnt Sienna. Add a bracelet and rings as illustrated.

4 Trace on the sceptre. Base with Rich Gold and highlight with Pale Gold. Follow the previous instructions for painting the jewels.

COLOUR KEY

1	Carbon Black	9	Pale Gold
2	DA Slate Grey	10	DA Flesh Tone
3	Colony Blue	11	DA Shading Flesh
4	Yellow Oxide	12	DA Sable Brown
5	Jade	13	Vermilion
6	Cobalt Blue	14	Burnt Sienna
7	Warm White	15	Burgundy
8	Rich Gold		

ROSE

1 Mix Burgundy with a touch of Warm White and base the rose. Shade the centre with Burgundy. Trace on the petal details.

2 Paint highlights with a sideload of Warm White.

3 Shade round the outside of the inner petals and around the inside of the outer petals with a sideload of Burgundy.

4 Add Jade sepal teardrop strokes and Yellow Oxide dots in the centre of the rose.

LETTERING

Using a 3mm (⅛in) flat brush, paint the lettering in Carbon Black.

FINISHING

Allow to dry for 24 hours. Then apply two or three coats of varnish. Allow to dry for 24 hours before antiquing with oil-based Burnt Umber (see page 23).

Elizabeth I

1

2

3

4

	1		4				10		13
	2		5		7		11		14
	3		6		8	9	12		15

FLORAL FOLK ART TIN KETTLE

THE FLORAL BUNCH PORTRAYED HERE WAS A VERY POPULAR DECORATIVE THEME THROUGHOUT MUCH OF EUROPE WHEN THE ERA OF FURNITURE PAINTING GOT UNDER WAY IN THE EIGHTEENTH CENTURY. THE FLAT SURFACES OF CUPBOARDS AND CHESTS WERE FAVOURITE AREAS TO ENLIVEN WITH FLOWERS. TO CREATE AN ATMOSPHERE OF ANTIQUITY, THE BRIGHTER COLOURS HAVE BEEN SUBDUED HERE WITH TIPPED AND UNDERMIXED EARTH COLOURS. GLIMPSES OF THE BLACK BACKGROUND SHOWING THROUGH THE STROKEWORK HEIGHTEN THE EFFECT.

Painting Style

This is a very traditional composition based on the most basic strokework shapes: commas, S strokes and C strokes. To avoid a look that is too contrived because after all we are trying to mimic rustic values, don't be tempted to wash your brush out too much. Build up the undermixed and tipped colours in various proportions rather than in precise formulas. Use the instructions given here as a loose guide rather than a rigid menu

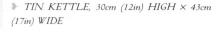

• m a t e r i a l s •

❦ *TIN KETTLE, 30cm (12in) HIGH × 43cm (17in) WIDE*

❦ BASE COAT
Black (Jo Sonja's background colour or similar substitute)

❦ FINISH
Sealer

❦ PALETTE
Smoked Pearl, Burnt Umber, Yellow Oxide, Warm White, Payne's Grey, DA Sand, Cadmium Yellow Light, Burnt Sienna, Cadmium Scarlet, Moss Green, Pine Green, Raw Umber

❦ BRUSHES
Large brush, 12mm (½ in) flat, No.4 round, No.6 round, liner, No.3 round

❦ OTHER SUPPLIES
Brown paper bag, tracing paper, graphite paper, chalk pencil

BASE COAT

1   Prepare the tin kettle following the instructions for preparation of new and old tin (see pages 19–20).
2   Using a large brush, apply three coats of Black background paint, sanding lightly between coats with a brown paper bag when dry.
3   Trace the pattern on to the kettle.

LARGE WHITE FLOWERS

1   Load a 12mm (½ in) flat brush with Smoked Pearl, sideloaded with Burnt Umber. Paint each petal using one or two crescent strokes as required, painting the one nearest the centre first.
2   Load a No.4 round brush with Yellow Oxide and paint the centre of the flower.
3   Load a No.6 round brush with Warm White and apply comma strokes skirting each petal.
4   Load a liner with Payne's Grey and outline the yellow centre. Add central cross-hatched lines.

SMALL WHITE FLOWERS

1   Flatten a No.4 round brush and load it with DA Sand. Paint the petals, using two overlapped strokes per petal. Begin with strokes at the outer edge and pull them into the centre. Wipe most of the paint off the brush.
2   With the same flattened brush, pick up a touch of Payne's Grey, and paint the centre of the flower.

SMALL YELLOW BELL FLOWER

1   Load a No.3 round brush with Cadmium Yellow Light tipped with Burnt Sienna and paint the central teardrop stroke.

2   Load the brush with the same two colours again and paint the two commas on either side of the teardrop stroke.
3   Load the brush with Yellow Oxide tipped with Burnt Sienna and paint comma accents.

ROSES

1   Load a 12mm (½ in) flat brush with Cadmium Scarlet. Paint the skirt petals using crescent strokes.
2   Load the brush with Cadmium Scarlet and touch the chisel into Burnt Umber. Use a circle stroke to paint the centre.
3   Load a No.3 round brush with Cadmium Scarlet tipped with Burnt Umber and paint commas on one edge of each skirting petal.
4   Load a No.6 round brush with Cadmium Scarlet tipped with Burnt Umber and use to paint commas on to the rose bowl.
5   Dot the centres with Yellow Oxide.

LARGE LEAVES

Refer to the coloured worksheet and note the dabs of undermixed paint using Moss Green, Pine Green and

COLOUR KEY
1   *Warm White*
2   *DA Sand*
3   *Smoked Pearl*
4   *Burnt Umber*
5   *Payne's Grey*
6   *Cadmium Yellow Light*
7   *Yellow Oxide*
8   *Burnt Sienna*
9   *Cadmium Scarlet*

LEAF COLOUR KEY
1   *Moss Green*
2   *Pine Green*
3   *Burnt Sienna*
4   *Burnt Umber*

Burnt Sienna. You don't need to clean off your brush and start again for each stroke. The mixture will begin to look blended as you apply the strokes, but this can be offset by touching the chisel and its side to one or more of the colours. Paint two leaf strokes per leaf. At the pointed ends of the leaves, add a stroke following the contours.

SEED PODS

1   With a No.4 round brush, mix Payne's Grey with Warm White, and paint the centre of each seed pod.
2   Using the undermixing method load a 12mm (½in) flat brush with Cadmium Scarlet, Moss Green, Burnt Sienna and Raw Umber, then paint the seed pod. Vary the effect on each one.
3   Add the white dots using the wooden end of the brush.
4   Paint the stem with Pine Green mixed with a little Moss Green using a liner.

TULIPS

1   Load a No.6 round brush with Yellow Oxide tipped with Burnt Sienna. Beginning at the bottom centre, paint two overlapping strokes to create the central portion of the tulip.

2   Then, reloading the brush with the same colours, add the side strokes.
3   Paint the tulip base with Payne's Grey mixed with Warm White. Add the stem as before.

WING FLOWERS

1   Load a 12mm (½in) flat brush with Yellow Oxide sideloaded with Burnt Umber. Paint crescent strokes on the wings.
2   Load a No.4 round brush with Yellow Oxide tipped with Burnt Sienna and Payne's Grey and paint two strokes in the centre.
3   Add the base with Payne's Grey and Warm White mixture.

LEAFY SPRIG

1   Use a liner to paint the stem with Pine Green mixed with a touch of Moss Green.
2   Paint the scroll stem. Use a loose shoulder motion.
3   Add the commas using Pine Green tipped with Moss Green and/or Burnt Sienna. Vary them as much as you can.

FINISHING

Allow the paint to dry for 24 hours, then apply a coat of sealer to protect the surface. Leave to dry.

WILLIAM MORRIS HATBOX

A RETURN TO CRAFTSMANSHIP AND SIMPLE DESIGN BASED ON NATURE AND MEDIEVAL GOTHIC STYLES WAS THE CALLING OF THE ARTS AND CRAFTS MOVEMENT LED BY WILLIAM MORRIS IN THE LATE NINETEENTH CENTURY. HENRY DEARLE, WHO WORKED FOR MORRIS & CO., CREATED 'ORCHARD' AS A WALLPAPER DESIGN, WHICH IS HERE ADAPTED FOR A HATBOX.

Painting Style

Stroke and linework are the main techniques used in this project. The orange leaves, for example, are simply a series of overlapping comma and S strokes leading from the base to the tip and then accentuated with sideloading and linework. The strokes in the broader leaves are laid in to suggest the movement

❧ *HATBOX, 45cm (18in) IN DIAMETER*

❧ **BASE COAT**
Teal Green

❧ **FINISH**
Water-based varnish

❧ **PALETTE**
Teal Green, Pale Gold, Rich Gold, Moss Green, Jade, Green Oxide, Smoked Pearl, Norwegian Orange, Burnt Sienna,

Burnt Umber, Turners Yellow, Warm White, Burgundy, Cobalt Blue

❧ **BRUSHES**
Large brush, No.3 round, No.4 liner, No.4 round, 12mm (½in) flat, 6mm (¼in) flat, 3mm (⅛in) flat

❧ **OTHER SUPPLIES**
Brown paper bag, tracing paper, graphite paper, chalk pencil, slow-drying medium, tape measure, masking tape, newspaper, ruler

BASE COAT

1　Using a large brush, apply two or three coats of Teal Green to all surfaces of the box and lid including the insides. Allow each coat to dry, then sand it with a brown paper bag, before applying the next coat. Allow to dry.

2　Trace the pattern on to the hatbox.

LID BORDER

Dilute Pale Gold with slow-drying medium to produce a transparent effect and to enable you to smooth in the strokes with the shape of the leaves.

1　Load a No.3 round brush with Pale Gold and lay in the central stroke first, followed by those on either side. Paint the leaf outlines, then fill in the whole leaf, moving the strokes with the leaf shapes. Allow to dry.

2　Load a liner with Rich Gold. Paint the veins and leaf outlines.

3　Pick up Pale Gold mixture with a liner and paint faint lines to band the leaves.

ORANGE BUNCHES

1　Use the No.4 round brush for all the leaves: Moss Green for the lighter toned leaves; Jade for the medium toned and Green Oxide for the darker toned. Alternate the tones to create balance.

2　Apply two coats of Smoked Pearl and Norwegian Orange mixed equally on the fruit. Shade between the leaves with a sideload of Teal Green and then shade around the base of all the leaves with the same colour. Shade the fruit with a sideload of Norwegian Orange.

3　Using a liner, add the central veins and smaller veins on the leaves in Teal Green. Outline each leaf in the same colour, then add an irregular dot in the centre of each orange.

TREE TRUNK AND BRANCHES

1　Mix an equal amount of Smoked Pearl with Burnt Sienna and paint the tree trunk and branches with a No.4 round brush.

2　Shade with a sideload of Burnt Umber using a 12mm (½in) flat brush.

WHITE BLOSSOMS

Dab the centre of each flower with Turners Yellow. Flatten a No.4 round brush and load it with Warm White, stroking it on the palette to dry it out. Paint the petals as illustrated. Repeat with Green Oxide for the leaves.

CANDY STRIPE BORDER FOR LID AND BOTTOM

1　Extend the tape measure around the circumference of the lid, positioning it 2cm (¾in) up from the bottom edge. Fasten with masking tape. Use the edge of the tape as a guideline for drawing a chalk line round the lid with a chalk pencil. Mark off 2.5cm (1in) segments all around the lid. Adjust the markings at the end if it does not measure out exactly right.

2　Load a 6mm (¼in) flat brush with Smoked Pearl and paint alternate 2.5cm (1in) segments. Angle the brush slightly as you paint. Then load the same brush with Jade and use it to paint the segments that are in between those painted with Smoked Pearl.

3   Repeat this procedure on the bottom edge of the base of the hatbox.

SIDE OF BOX BASE

1   Fasten together several sheets of newspaper with masking tape; there should be enough to go around the box base. Fold the newspaper into a long strip measuring 11cm (4¼in) in width. Trim the paper where the two ends meet.

2   Remove the strip. Fold it in half lengthwise, then into quarters, and finally into eighths. Crease the folds well. Unfold the strip. Then, with a ruler and pencil, join up the fold points as indicated on the diagram to make diamond segments. Wrap the strip around the box again and secure it with masking tape. Use the top and bottom edges as a guideline and go around it with a chalk pencil. Trace on the diamonds.

3   Load a No.4 liner with Jade and paint along the guidelines. Where the diamonds meet, make dots in the same colour, using the wooden end of the brush.

4   Position the four floral motifs in the centre of each diamond in the following order: primula, daisy, bluebell, tulip x 2.

PRIMULA

Paint crescent strokes for the petals using a 6mm (¼in) flat brush loaded with Burgundy and a touch of Warm White. Then paint the comma stroke leaves in Jade.

DAISY

Load and coat a liner with Warm White. Touch on the petals and paint the stem and leaves with Jade.

BLUEBELL

Use a teardrop and two comma strokes for the flower petals, using Cobalt Blue tipped with Warm White; use Jade for the stem.

TULIP

Use a teardrop and two comma strokes in Turners Yellow for the flower, and use Jade with a touch of Moss Green for the stem and leaves.

LETTERING

Mix Warm White in high concentration with slow-drying medium and paint the lettering using a 3mm (⅛in) flat brush. When dry, overpaint with Teal Green glaze to dampen down the Warm White.

FINISHING

Allow the hatbox to dry for 24 hours. Apply two or three coats of water-based varnish over the top and sides, sanding lightly between coats when dry.

COLOUR KEY

1   Teal Green
2   Norwegian Orange
3   Warm White
4   Moss Green
5   Jade
6   Burgundy
7a   Pale Gold
7b   Rich Gold
8   Green Oxide
9   Smoked Pearl
10   Cobalt Blue
11   Turners Yellow
12   Burnt Sienna
13   Burnt Umber

FOLD   FOLD   FOLD   FOLD   FOLD   FOLD   FOLD   FOLD

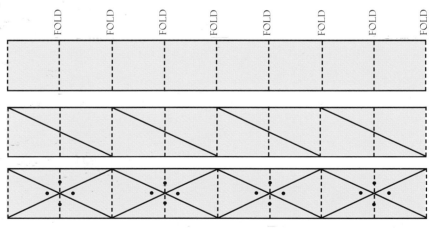

GUSTAVIAN TABLE WITH COCKERELS

THIS PROJECT ILLUSTRATES DECORATIVE PAINTING AT ITS SIMPLEST AND MOST TRADITIONAL. THE TREE OF LIFE THEME APPEARS IN MOST CULTURES. IN CHRISTIAN LANDS, AN URN PLANTED WITH OUTSIZED FLORALS SYMBOLIZES RENEWAL, GROWTH AND VITALITY. THE ADDITION OF THE BIRDS IS TO REMIND US OF ITS WATER-GIVING PROPERTIES. RESURRECTION IS IMPLIED BY THE COCKERELS.

Painting Style

This project falls within our description of traditional folk art painting because it relies exclusively on strokework. In the cockerel's tail, large comma strokes are combined with a series of sideloaded flat S strokes, while C strokes form the leaves and tulip petals. The monochromatic design is painted using Payne's Grey and is complemented by blue trim on an antiqued glazed background. This colour scheme is so subtle that the boldness of the design will fit into most room settings without being overwhelming

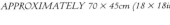

• m a t e r i a l s •

❧ *GUSTAVIAN TABLE,*
APPROXIMATELY 70 × 45cm (18 × 18in)

❧ **BASE COAT**
Dove Grey (Jo Sonja's background
colour or similar substitute)
Burnt Umber

❧ **FINISH**
Water-based varnish

❧ **PALETTE**
Payne's Grey, DA Baby Blue, DA French
Grey Blue

❧ **BRUSHES**
Large brush, 12mm (½ in) flat, 6mm
(¼ in) flat, No.8 round, No.4 round, liner

❧ **OTHER SUPPLIES**
Fine sandpaper, clear glazing medium,
slow-drying medium (optional), tracing
paper, chalk pencil, adhesive tape, knead-
able eraser

BASE COAT

1   Using a large brush, base-coat the table with
three coats of Dove Grey Background Colour.
Allow each coat to dry, sand lightly, then apply the
next coat.

2   Dispense clear glazing medium into a small jar
to a depth of 2.5–5cm (1–2in). Add 1–2 drops of
Burnt Umber into the medium and mix well. Test
the colour against the painted instruction panel.
Add more pigment or medium if necessary. You
may want to add some slow-drying medium to this
mixture to delay the drying time, thus allowing
more time to work the application of glazing.

3   To glaze the table top, smooth all strokes across
the widest part of the table. Now glaze each side,
smoothing the mixture across the aprons and down
the legs. Allow the glaze to dry completely.

4   Transfer the pattern on to the front apron.

5   Mix Baby Blue and French Grey Blue in the
proportion of 3:1. Using a 12mm (½ in) flat brush,
paint the trim around the table top's bevelled edge
and along the apron edges, sides, front and back.

TREE OF LIFE, URN AND COCKERELS

1   Using Payne's Grey for the whole design, start
by painting the cockerels. First paint four overlapping sideloaded curves with a 6mm (¼ in) flat brush.
Then apply the four comma strokes with a No.8
round brush.

2   Following the colour instruction sheet and using
a 6mm (¼ in) flat brush, add the top row of curves,
then the middle row, and finally the bottom row of
reverse curves.

3   Using the sideload method follow the cockerel
outlines. Base-in the feet; dot the eye with the
wooden end of the brush.

4   Using a No.4 round brush, paint all the liner
strokes on the tree of life as illustrated bottom left;
paint all the strokes as illustrated bottom right.

5   Using a 6mm (¼ in) flat brush, outline everything else with the sideload method as illustrated in
the centre of the glazed panel. Place hatching in the
centre of the florals with a liner.

FINISHING

Allow to dry for 24
hours, then erase tracing
lines and apply two or
three coats of water-
based varnish, sanding
very lightly between
coats once dry.

COLOUR KEY

1   *Dove Grey*
2   *Burnt Umber*
3   *Baby Blue*
4   *French Grey Blue*
5   *Payne's Grey*

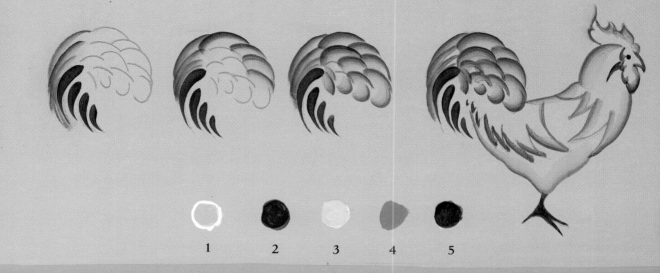

1   2   3   4   5

CACHEPOT WITH ROSES AND TOBACCO PLANT

*B*OTANICAL ILLUSTRATION, ESPECIALLY EXAMPLES PAINTED BY PIERRE JOSEPH REDOUTÉ (1759–1840), IS OFTEN FEATURED ON CLASSICAL OBJECTS. REDOUTÉ STANDS OUT AMONG BOTANICAL ILLUSTRATORS FOR HIS EXQUISITE USE OF COLOUR AND THE STRONG DECORATIVE FEELING HE CONVEYS IN WORK WHICH IS OSTENSIBLY CARRIED OUT FOR SCIENTIFIC RECORDS. THIS ROSE DESIGN IS A COPY OF ONE OF HIS ILLUSTRATIONS. THE TOBACCO PLANT IS A DESIGN I DEVELOPED WHILE PAINTING IN THE UMBRIAN COUNTRYSIDE OF ITALY. WHILE NOT A BOTANICAL ILLUSTRATION IN THE STRICTEST SENSE, IT CONVEYS THAT SORT OF IMPRESSION. THE TWO DESIGNS WORK WELL IN PARTNERSHIP: THE MOST CHERISHED FLOWER AND MOST DREADED WEED – BUT SUCH A BEAUTIFUL WEED!

❦

Painting Style
In this project the blending technique
(used for the rose) and the strokework technique
(used for the tobacco plant) are combined

• m a t e r i a l s •

▸ CACHEPOT, 28cm × 20cm (11½in × 8in)

▸ BASE COAT
Primrose (Jo Sonja's background colour or similar substitute)

▸ FINISH
Water-based varnish

▸ PALETTE
Warm White, Smoked Pearl, Fawn, Yellow Oxide, Rich Gold, Carbon Black, DA Dusty Rose, Moss Green, Rose Pink, Pine Green, Burgundy, Teal Green, Payne's Grey, Turners Yellow, Burnt Sienna, DA Hauser Light Green

▸ BRUSHES
Large brush, No.3 round, 12mm (½in) flat, 6mm (¼in) flat

▸ OTHER SUPPLIES
Brown paper bag, tracing paper, graphite paper, chalk pencil, ruler, masking tape, slow-drying medium

BASE COAT

1   Using a large brush, apply two or three coats of Primrose background colour over the cachepot, allowing each coat to dry and then sanding with a brown paper bag before applying the next coat.

2   Transfer the cameo outlines on the pot (see page 24). Apply three coats of Warm White over the transferred pattern. Allow to dry.

3   Saturate the brush with slow-drying medium and mix this with a small amount of Smoked Pearl. Apply over the white area, leaving a margin of 5cm (2in) all the way around. Use a flattened round brush along the paint edge to tease the paint out until it fades into the white background.

4   Load a No.3 round brush with Fawn and paint an S stroke border around the outer edge of the cameo. Load the same brush with Yellow Oxide and paint over every alternate Fawn S stroke.

5   Paint two or three coats of Rich Gold on the top edges of the pot to create a trim.

6   Load a 12mm (½ in) flat brush with Carbon Black. Place the broad side of the brush along the right angles of all edges in turn, then draw it along the full length of each edge. This technique is an easy way to line right-angled edges.

ROSE

Use slow-drying medium for all applications, and mix the medium with tiny amounts of paint. Flatten the brush, squeezing out most of the loaded mixture before painting.

1   Base-in the rose with DA Dusty Rose mixture using a No.3 round brush. Then base-in the leaves and stem with Moss Green mixture.

2   Add a tiny amount of Rose Pink to the DA Dusty Rose mixture and shade in places as illustrated with the same brush. Apply Pine Green mixture to the leaves.

3   Add a tiny amount of Burgundy to the pink mixture and apply deeper shading on the petals as illustrated. Sideload a 6mm (¼ in) flat brush with Teal Green mixture and shade as illustrated.

4   Sideload a 6mm (¼ in) flat brush with Burgundy mixture and a touch of Payne's Grey and stroke this around the petals as illustrated. Load a liner with Teal Green mixture and very lightly add the vein lines and faint jagged outlines on the leaves.

FLOWER CENTRES

1   Use a flattened No.3 brush and dab Turners Yellow into each flower centre.

2   Sideload a flat brush with Warm White and paint round the centre edge. Sideload Moss Green and paint the bull's eye in the centre.

3   Flatten a No.3 round brush, pick up a tiny amount of Burnt Sienna mixture and pat it round the edge as illustrated. Add a few darker dots with the tip of a liner.

4   Finally, add a few faint lines.

TOBACCO PLANT

Paint all leaves with two strokes using a 6mm (¼ in) flat brush. Dilute the paint with water rather than with slow-drying medium.

1   Load the brush with DA Hauser Light Green. Beginning at the bottom of the leaf, paint the left half of the left central leaf, then the right half. A slight wobbling movement as you paint up the stem produces an undulating leafy look. Don't wash out the brush.

2   On one corner of the same brush, pick up and blend a small amount of Pine Green. Paint the right central leaf, right and left halves.

3   Wash out the brush then load it with DA Hauser Light Green and paint the top halves of leaves on each side of the central leaves. Don't wash out the brush. Pick up Pine Green and mix, then paint the bottom halves of these leaves. Wash out the brush.

4   Load the brush with DA Hauser Light Green and paint the last two leaves.

5   Load a No.3 round brush with undermixed DA Hauser Light Green and Pine Green and then paint the stem.

6   With the flat brush, mix the same colours and paint a half-heart stroke at the top of the stem, followed by two more going down the stem in dry-brushed half-hearts.

7   With the No.3 round brush, mix Teal Green with Pine Green and paint three dark comma strokes on the stem.

FINISHING

Allow the cachepot to dry for 24 hours, then apply a coat of water-based varnish over the surface to protect the paint.

TRAY IN PONTYPOOL STYLE

In the late seventeenth century, the Allgood family of Pontypool, Wales, developed a process which could mimic lacquerware from the Far East. It was so versatile that it could be applied to a range of surfaces, including tin and papier mâché. The inspiration for this project comes from a selection of motifs which appear on various pieces of Pontypool ware in the Cardiff City Museum collection in Wales.

Painting Style

The inside border of the tray is basic strokework; the outside, meandering border that looks like worm tracks is a classic pattern called 'Stormont' which is painted with a liner. The central cameo, surprisingly, uses bold rather than blended painting techniques and is suitable for even the less experienced painter

materials

CLASSIC OVAL TRAY, 48cm (19in) LONG

BASE COAT
Gold Oxide

FINISH
Satin water-based varnish

PALETTE
Gold Oxide, Pale Gold, Raw Umber, Warm White, Cobalt Blue, Cadmium Yellow, Smoked Pearl, DA Base Flesh, DA Baby Blue

BRUSHES
Large brush, liner, No.3 round, No.4 round, 6mm (¼in) flat

OTHER SUPPLIES
Sealer, brown paper bag, ruler, light chalk pencil, tracing paper, graphite paper, slow-drying medium, masking tape, Burnt Umber artist's oil colour, soft cloth

BASE COAT

Using a large brush, apply one coat of sealer over the tray, and allow to dry. Now apply three coats of Gold Oxide, allowing each coat to dry then sanding lightly with a brown paper bag.

OUTER BORDER

1 To measure out the outside oval border, use a ruler and mark points at 2.5cm (1in) intervals around the edge with a light chalk pencil. Join up the marks. For the inside oval border, measure and mark off points 5cm (2in) apart in the same way.

2 The meander pattern consists of wobbling Ys which alternate between being upright and upside-down. Transfer the pattern on the tray (see page 24) or paint it freehand. Load a liner with slow-drying medium and Pale Gold and paint the border design.

INNER BORDER

1 Centralize the inside border pattern on the tray and trace in position. Use masking tape to secure the tracing paper.

2 Load a liner with Pale Gold and paint the dominant S strokes as illustrated.

3 Using a liner, paint the diminishing comma strokes on the upper side of each frond in Raw Umber, then paint the lower ones in the same colour. Now add the Pale Gold central vein, also with a liner.

4 Paint the Warm White and Cobalt Blue flowers as illustrated. Around each flower, paint curlicues on either side. Paint loosely, from the shoulder. Add Cadmium Yellow dots around the centres of the white flowers.

5 Draw a chalk line round the outside edge of the entire inner border, and then line this with Pale Gold.

CUPID PATTERN

1 Centralize the cupid pattern on the tray and trace on the outside pattern edge. Apply three coats of Smoked Pearl using a No.3 round brush, then trace on the cupids and clouds.

2 Moisten a No.4 round brush with slow-drying medium and pick up DA Base Flesh, then paint the

body, head and hair of each cupid. Moisten the brush with slow-drying medium and pick up Warm White, then paint the wings and clouds. Dry with a hair dryer.

3 Add a second coat of these colours. Add the outlines with a liner. Dilute Raw Umber to a light tone with slow-drying medium. Roll the liner through it into a point, then apply light outlines using the very tip of the brush. If you look carefully at the illustration, you will notice that it is composed of a series of S strokes. By using slow-drying medium, outlines you are not happy with can easily be removed with a damp brush and then repainted if necessary.

4 Load a liner with undermixed Raw Umber and slow-drying medium and use it to paint the sprig that the cupid is holding. The sprig is composed of a series of comma strokes which start from the top.

5 Moisten a 6mm (¼ in) flat brush with slow-drying medium and sideload with Raw Umber. Apply the shading to the underarms, the lower part of the legs, the sides of faces, the right wing on the right cupid, hair, and clouds.

6 Moisten the same brush again and sideload with Warm White. Apply highlighting to the upper arms, legs, thighs, bottom and hair, as shown.

7 Sideload DA Baby Blue highlights as illustrated.

8 Line the outer edge of this patterned oval with Pale Gold. With a chalk pencil, draw a second outline approximately 6mm (¼ in) from the first oval outline, then line with Pale Gold.

FINISHING

After allowing to dry for 24 hours, apply two or three coats of satin water-based varnish over the tray. Allow to dry. Finally, complete with an antique finish (see page 23).

COLOUR KEY

1 Gold Oxide
2 Smoked Pearl
3 Pale Gold
4 Raw Umber
5 Warm White
6 Cobalt Blue
7 Cadmium Yellow
8 DA Baby Blue
9 DA Base Flesh

CHARLES RENNIE MACKINTOSH UMBRELLA STAND

*T*HE SCOTTISH ARCHITECT AND DESIGNER CHARLES RENNIE MACKINTOSH (1868–1928) WAS WELL KNOWN IN EUROPE AT THE TURN OF THE CENTURY FOR HIS RECTILINEAR VERSION OF ART NOUVEAU. HIS WIFE, THE DESIGNER MARGARET MACDONALD, WORKED CLOSELY WITH HIM IN A SIMILAR STYLE. ONE OF HIS DESIGNS FOR A HOUSE, CALLED 'HOUSE FOR AN ART LOVER', WAS ACTUALLY BUILT IN GLASGOW IN THE 1990S. A COMMISSION OF PANELS FOR THE HOUSE, IN THE SPIRIT OF THE WORK OF MARGARET MACDONALD, CREATED BY JENNY AND DAI VAUGHN, WAS THE DIRECT INSPIRATION FOR THIS DESIGN FOR AN UMBRELLA STAND.

• m a t e r i a l s •

❧ *UMBRELLA STAND, 20cm × 30cm × 60cm (8in × 12in × 24in)*

❧ BASE COAT
Soft White (Jo Sonja's background colour or similar substitute)

❧ FINISH
Black (Jo Sonja's background colour or similar substitute), water-based varnish

❧ PALETTE
Dioxin Purple, Payne's Grey, Raw Umber, Pine Green, Brilliant Green, Rose Pink

❧ BRUSHES
Large brush, No.4 round, liner, 6mm (¼in) flat, No.8 round, No.3 round

❧ OTHER SUPPLIES
Brown paper bag, tracing paper, graphite paper, chalk pencil, ruler, DecoArt Dimensions Easy Writer x 2 or similar substitute, slow-drying medium, soft cloth, surgical or methylated spirits (rubbing or denatured alcohol)

BASE COAT

1   Using a large brush, apply two coats of Soft White background paint over the whole umbrella stand, sanding between coats with a brown paper bag when dry.

2   Transfer the pattern on to the umbrella stand (see page 24). Use a ruler for the straight lines.

3   Using DA Dimensions Easy Writer, outline the transferred pattern, excluding the face, shoulders and hands. (Don't worry if your lines are uneven. Hiccups, wobbles or skipped parts of lines are not crucial. If you make a real blunder, scrape it off with a palette knife and start again.) Allow to dry overnight. It will still feel pliable to the touch.

4   Apply one or two more coats of Soft White background colour over the stand, including the embossed lines. You can use a hair dryer for drying.

5   To paint within the lines, mix slow-drying medium with small amounts of paint. Work from the blending palette by blending two brush-loads of slow-drying medium using a No.4 round brush. Then introduce small amounts of pigment until you match the tones on the colour work sheet. Paint in the following order:

MAUVE AREAS

Apply two coats, including the jewel-like spots, using Dioxin Purple with a touch of Payne's Grey.

BROWN AREAS

Using Raw Umber and a No.3 round brush, build up the coats on the hair until it is medium brown. Use a No.4 round brush for the robe.

GREEN AREAS

Mix Pine Green and Brilliant Green in the ratio of approximately 2:1. Apply two or more coats on the darker areas, including the jewel-like spots. Use a No.3 round brush for the smaller areas and a No.8 round for the larger ones.

ROSE PINK

Apply this colour as illustrated.

6   Around the bottom side sections of the robe, apply first a coat of Raw Umber, then a coat of Pine Green mixed with Brilliant Green for some gentle colour differentiation, using a No.8 round brush. To add texture, dampen a soft cloth with surgical or methylated spirit and brush lightly over the robe, the upper mauve section and the deeper green section.

7   Stand back from your piece and decide if the embossed line is too discreet. If so, roll a liner to a sharp point in slow-drying medium and Raw Umber, then line along both sides of each embossed line.

FACE AND HANDS

1   Reposition the pattern and transfer the outlines of the hands and face (see page 24).

2   Roll a liner in slow-drying medium and Raw Umber to a point. Paint the hand and face outlines as illustrated, including the bottom eye line.

3   Using a liner, paint the lips with Rose Pink.

4   Sideload a 6mm (¼ in) flat brush with the merest touch of Rose Pink, blend, then touch it into the wet brown mixture used above. Apply the faint upper eye line and the cheek line.

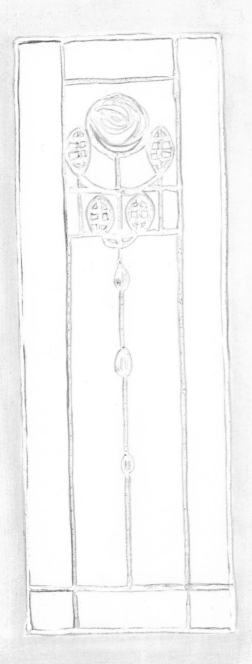

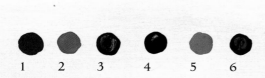

COLOUR KEY

1   Pine Green
2   Brilliant Green
3   Raw Umber
4   Payne's Grey
5   Rose Pink
6   Dioxin Purple

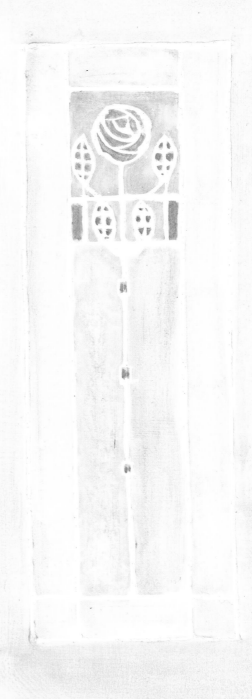

Painting Style

⬤ *This is an example of bold painting. The graphic simplicity and clarity of the design lend themselves well to the technique. Instead of using a brush or pen for outlines as a final stage, we begin by making embossed outlines (using DecoArt Dimensions Easy Writer) on to which paint is applied* ⬤

 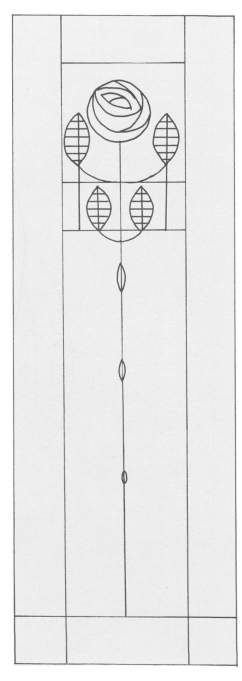

FINISHING

1   Using a large brush, paint two or three coats of Black background paint on the inside of the stand.
2   Paint the black outline on the bevelled edges at top and bottom of the stand with a No.8 round brush.
3   Allow to dry for 24 hours, then apply two or three coats of water-based varnish, allowing each coat to dry before applying the next.

GRACE BARNSLEY TEAWARE DESIGN

GRACE BARNSLEY, A DESIGNER AND POTTERY PAINTRESS FOR WEDGWOOD AROUND THE YEARS OF WORLD WAR I, WAS THE DAUGHTER OF SIDNEY BARNSLEY, A LEADING FIGURE IN THE ARTS AND CRAFTS MOVEMENT. TYPICAL OF THE TIMES, THE BARNSLEY FAMILY'S QUEST FOR SIMPLICITY AND HAND-CRAFTSMANSHIP LED THEM TO LIVE AND WORK IN THE BEAUTIFUL COTSWOLD LANDSCAPE OF ENGLAND, AMONG A COMMUNITY WHOSE CRAFTED WARES HAVE BECOME PART OF THE NATIONAL ARCHIVE. THE EXQUISITELY SIMPLE MOTIF WHICH APPEARS HERE WAS FIRST PAINTED BY GRACE ON A WEDGWOOD TEAPOT, WHICH IS NOW DISPLAYED IN THE CHELTENHAM CITY ART MUSEUM, ENGLAND.

• m a t e r i a l s •

❧ *PAPIER MÂCHÉ BOX, APPROXIMATELY 24cm (9 ½ in) IN DIAMETER*

❧ BASE COAT
Soft White (Jo Sonja's background colour or similar substitute)

❧ FINISH
Satin varnish

❧ PALETTE
DA Boysenberry Pink, Green Oxide, Burnt Sienna, Cadmium Scarlet

❧ BRUSHES
Large brush, No.4 round, liner

❧ OTHER SUPPLIES
Brown paper bag, tracing paper, graphite paper, chalk pencil, masking tape, eraser, slow-drying medium

To encourage the strokes to look as transparent as they would on pottery or porcelain, use slow-drying medium instead of water as a thinner.

BASE COAT
Using a large brush, apply two or three coats of Soft White background paint over the box, sanding between coats with a brown paper bag when dry.

FLOWERS AND LEAVES
1   Transfer the pattern on to the box.
2   Load a No.4 round brush with DA Boysenberry Pink and paint the central top stroke, followed by the sets of three on each side.
3   Paint the left- and right-hand sets in the same way. Note that these are groups of five strokes, whereas the uppermost set was a group of seven.
4   Paint the leaves with Green Oxide.
5   Load a liner with Burnt Sienna and paint the flower centre, branches and main stem.
6   Dip the wooden end of the brush into Cadmium Scarlet and apply the dots.

LID
Using the wooden end of the brush, apply Cadmium Scarlet dots to the lid at 12mm (½ in) intervals.

FINISHING
1   Allow the paint to dry for 24 hours, then erase the tracing lines.
2   Apply two or three coats of satin varnish, sanding lightly with a brown paper bag between coats when dry.

Painting Style

● *Traditional strokework and linework are the essence of this simple design, which has been adapted to decorate a papier mâché box* ●

COLOUR KEY
1   *DA Boysenberry Pink*
2   *Green Oxide*
3   *Burnt Sienna*
4   *Cadmium Scarlet*

1   2   3   4

COCKEREL TILES

THIS COCKEREL IS A STROKEWORK MEDLEY OF VIBRANT COLOUR PAINTED ON TILES. THE TOOTH OF THE CERAMIC TILE, UNLIKE THE SMOOTH SURFACE OF MEDIUM DENSITY FIBREBOARD (MDF), GIVES A TEXTURE TO THE PAINT, MAKING IT APPEAR TO CATCH THE LIGHT, SIMILAR TO PAINTING ON A GRAINED WATER-COLOUR PAPER. NO HEAT SETTING IS REQUIRED TO FIX THE PIGMENT ON TO THE TILES BECAUSE I HAVE USED THE MOST UP-TO-DATE TILE MEDIUMS.

Painting Style

This project uses strokework techniques; the contemporary look is produced by building up suggested stroke shapes with a varied colour palette. Placement of each stroke does not have to be precise. A feel for movement and direction of the plumes by painting in line with body shape is what you should be aiming for

1

2

3

4

5

6

7

8

• m a t e r i a l s •

❧ *4 TERRACOTTA TILES, 15cm (5¼ in)*
SQUARE

❧ **BASE COAT**
Glass and tile primer (Jo Sonja's primer
or similar substitute)

❧ **FINISH**
Gloss varnish

❧ **PALETTE**
Napthol Red Light, Turners Yellow,
Norwegian Orange, DA Uniform Blue,
DA Dusty Rose, DA Mint Julep Green,

Cadmium Yellow Light, Storm Blue,
Cobalt Blue, Burnt Sienna, Payne's Grey

❧ **BRUSHES**
Large brush, No.6 round, No.4 round,
liner

❧ **OTHER SUPPLIES**
Plyboard 30cm (11½ in) square, tile
adhesive, tile grout, spatula, cloth,
tracing paper, graphite paper, chalk
pencil, glass and tile painting medium
(Jo Sonja's medium or similar substitute),
eraser

PREPARING THE TILES

1   Glue the tiles to the plyboard with tile adhesive. Allow to dry.
2   Apply grout between the tiles with a spatula. Remove excess grout with a cloth. Allow to dry.
3   Using a large brush, apply one coat of glass and tile primer. Allow to dry.
4   Trace the pattern on the painted tiles.

COCKEREL

Prepare each pigment by mixing each colour with glass and tile painting medium in the ratio of 1:3.
1   Using the colour worksheets 1–8 as your guide, stroke on the pigments in their prescribed order, using a No.6 round brush for the larger strokes and a No.4 round brush for the smaller strokes. First paint the comb in Napthol Red Light, the beak in Turners Yellow, and the base plumes in Norwegian Orange.
2   Next, paint the breast and tail plumes in DA Uniform Blue, and the feet in DA Dusty Rose.
3   Paint the body overstrokes with Napthol Red Light, DA Mint Julep Green and DA Dusty Rose.
4   Use Turners Yellow and Cadmium Yellow Light undermixed to apply additional overstrokes on the body.
5   Use Storm Blue for the tail plumes.
6   Add tail strokes and additional body strokes in Cobalt Blue.
7   Add additional tail strokes in Burnt Sienna. Then replace the pattern and retrace the wings.
8   Use Payne's Grey to paint the final tail plumes, outlining the wings, body, comb, legs, beak and eye detail.

COLOUR KEY

1 *Napthol Red Light,*
   Norwegian Orange,
   Turners Yellow
2 *DA Uniform Blue,*
   DA Dusty Rose
3 *Napthol Red Light,*
   DA Mint Julep
   Green, DA Dusty

   Rose
4 *Turners Yellow,*
   Cadmium Yellow
   Light
5 *Storm Blue*
6 *Cobalt Blue*
7 *Burnt Sienna*
8 *Payne's Grey*

FINISHING

1   Allow to dry for two weeks. Then erase the tracing lines.
2   Varnish the painted tiles with gloss varnish and leave to dry.

EDWARDIAN TRAY WITH ANEMONES

During the Victorian and Edwardian periods, a must for any young lady of the 'genteel' classes was to learn to paint floral decoration. Some of the floral patterns were quite elaborate and beautifully painted in a realistic strokework style. This is an adaptation from an Edwardian tray I restored for a friend.

Painting Style

There is no sideloading or blending used in this pattern as you might expect, just simple strokework of a suggestive nature to create a fluent painterly look while maximizing the use of the dark background. The brush is loaded with very little paint, and some dry-brushing is also used. The main thing is to aim for freshness by resisting too many strokes

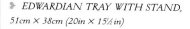

materials

❧ *EDWARDIAN TRAY WITH STAND,*
51cm × 38cm (20in × 15½ in)

❧ BASE COAT
Carbon Black

❧ FINISH
Water-based varnish

❧ PALETTE
DA Neutral Grey, DA Lavender, Napthol Red Light, Nimbus Grey, Scarlet, Warm White, DA Shading Flesh,

Green Oxide, Brilliant Green, Burnt Sienna, Cobalt Blue, Aqua, Pine Green, DA Flesh Tone, Turners Yellow, Moss Green, Rich Gold (optional)

❧ BRUSHES
Large brush, No.3 round, No.4 round, liner

❧ OTHER SUPPLIES
Tracing paper, graphite paper, chalk pencil, brown paper bag, glazing medium (optional)

BASE COAT

Apply three coats of Carbon Black background paint, sanding between coats with a brown paper bag when dry.

FLOWERS

On the colour worksheet, each floral grouping has some colour swatches beside it. For the anemones, the first swatch grouping is the colourway for the mauve flower; below it is the colourway for the red flower; below it is the colourway for the white flower; and finally the colourway for the leaves and stem. A No.3 and a No.4 round brush are used almost exclusively in a flattened form.

ANEMONES

1   Using a No.4 round brush, base each petal, beginning with the back central petals, and working towards those which appear to overlap. Paint the front petals last. Work from the outer edges into the centre except for the front petals which resemble commas. For the mauve petals, use DA Neutral Grey with a little DA Lavender. For the red flower, use Napthol Red Light. For the white flower, use Nimbus Grey.

2   Flatten the hairs of the brush to add some lighter stroke tones by lightly brushing over the base strokes. For the mauve flower, add a little Nimbus Grey to the mauve colours. For the red flower, use Scarlet. For the white flower, use Warm White. Then paint in the centre of each flower with a darker mauve tone, using the same colour for each of the anemones.

3   With a flattened No.3 round brush, apply lighter highlights on to the mauve and red anemones with Warm White. Using a liner, add light lines around the centres, pulling strokes out from the centre. On the white flower, repeat using DA Shading Flesh.

4   Around the centre area, use a brush to suggest dots in dark mauve, the same colour as the centre itself. Then use a liner to suggest light highlights on some of the petals. Pat a tiny amount of Green Oxide into the flower centres.

5   Load a liner with Green Oxide and paint comma stroke leaves. Don't clean the brush. Pick up some Brilliant Green and blend, then add some lighter commas over the darker strokes. Don't clean the brush. Roll it into a little Burnt Sienna, then paint the stem.

BLUEBELLS

1   Using a liner loaded with an equal mix of Cobalt Blue and DA Lavender, first make a tear-drop stroke in the middle, followed by two commas on either side. Don't wash out the brush.

2   Pick up a small amount of Aqua, blend on the palette, tip with a tiny amount of white, then paint the highlight on to the bells.

3   Undermix Cobalt Blue and DA Lavender and paint the bell buds, varying the mixture for each of them for contrast.

4   Highlight the points of the bells with paint in a light tone.

5   Load a liner with Pine Green and paint the leaves and stems.

PINK FLOWERS

1 Using a No.4 round brush, base the flowers with a mix of DA Shading Flesh and DA Lavender.
2 Flatten the brush and load with DA Shading Flesh. Dry-brush on some highlights.
3 Using a flattened No.4 round brush, dry-brush on DA Flesh Tone. Add lighter toned comma strokes to the petal tips.
4 Using the same tone as on the tips, make tiny sit-down teardrops for stamens.
5 Paint the greenery following the same method as for the anemones.

STRAWBERRIES

1 Using a No.3 round brush, base the flowers in Nimbus Grey, and the berries in Napthol Red Light. Use a light green tone for the leaf at the base of the stem.
2 Load a liner with Green Oxide and paint the central vein of the leaves. Then add the series of comma strokes, beginning at the outer edge and moving into the centre. Add dots on the straw-berries in Turners Yellow.
3 With a flattened No.3 round brush, dab a high-light of white into the petals as illustrated. Dab in the flower centre.

YELLOW FLOWERS

1 Load a No.3 round brush with Moss Green. Use sit-down strokes, joining up the tails at the petal bases.
2 Highlight these petals with varying tones of Warm White mixed with Turners Yellow.
3 Dab the centres with Brilliant Green, then over-lay with some smaller yellow-toned dots.
4 Roll a liner in Burnt Sienna and paint the flower stems.

COLOUR KEY

ANEMONES
1 DA Neutral Grey
2 DA Lavender
3 Nimbus Grey
4 DA Shading Flesh
5 Napthol Red Light
6 Scarlet
7 Warm White
8 Nimbus Grey
9 Warm White
10 DA Flesh Tone
11 Green Oxide
12 Warm White
13 Burnt Sienna

BLUEBELLS
1 DA Lavender
2 Cobalt Blue
3 Aqua
4 Warm White
5 Pine Green

LARGE PINK FLOWERS
1 DA Lavender
2 DA Shading Flesh

3 DA Flesh Tone
4 Green Oxide
5 Warm White

SMALL PINKS
1 DA Lavender
2 DA Shading Flesh
3 DA Flesh Tone
4 Green Oxide

YELLOW FLOWERS
1 Turners Yellow
2 Warm White
3 Brilliant Green
4 Moss Green
5 Burnt Sienna

STRAWBERRIES
1 Nimbus Grey
2 Warm White
3 Napthol Red Light
4 Turners Yellow
5 Moss Green
6 Green Oxide

FINISHING

Allow the tray to dry for 24 hours. Erase the tracing lines and apply two or three coats of varnish, allow-ing each coat to dry before applying the next. If you would like to add a trim, mix a bit of Rich Gold with glazing medium and apply with your fingertips around the edge, after varnishing.

ART DECO CHEST

 P̶AINTED IN THE SPIRIT OF ART DECO, THIS CHEST EVOKES THE JAZZY MOOD OF THE PERIOD WITH ITS LARGE STYLIZED FLORALS AGAINST A STRIKING SILVER BACKGROUND. THE DEER OR ANTELOPE WAS ALSO A POPULAR IMAGE AT THIS TIME. THIS ADAPTATION IS BASED ON THE DESIGN BY JEAN DUNAND, A FAMOUS FRENCH LACQUER PAINTER OF THE PERIOD.

Painting Style

This project has been painted in the bold tradition. The structure of the design relies on outlines which are filled in by glazes in light, medium and dark tones, never totally obscuring the silver background. The simple detailing added as final touches is stroked on. Sideloaded shades and highlights bring the deer to life

materials

▶ *WOODEN CHEST, 36cm × 22cm × 20cm (14in × 9in × 8in)*

▶ BASE COAT
All-purpose medium (Jo Sonja's medium or similar substitute), non-tarnishing Silver

▶ FINISH
Water-based varnish

▶ PALETTE
Carbon Black, Pale Gold, Payne's Grey, Warm White, Cobalt Blue, Cadmium Scarlet

▶ BRUSHES
Large brush, liner, No.3 round, No.3 mop (optional), No.4 round, 12mm (½in) flat

▶ OTHER SUPPLIES
Brown paper bag, tracing paper, graphite paper, chalk pencil, black brush pen (optional), slow-drying medium, sheet of acetate (optional), eraser, stylus, ruler

BASE COAT

1   Remove handles from the chest before you begin. Using a large brush, apply one coat of all-purpose medium over the chest. When dry, sand with a brown paper bag. Then apply two or three coats of non-tarnishing Silver pigment, sanding between coats when dry, once again using a brown paper bag.

2   The florals should range in size, so have some reductions and enlargements made at a print shop. Arrange the patterns randomly on the box, avoiding the area where the main design will be painted.

Trace in position, using my arrangement as an approximate guide.

3   Using either a black brush pen or a liner loaded with Carbon Black, apply all the floral outlines. If the liner is moistened with slow-drying medium instead of water, you will have plenty of time to remove mistakes. Dry with a hair dryer as you paint to avoid smudges. Brush-penned lines will smudge easily unless completely dried over several days, but if you place a sheet of acetate over the fresh paintwork and lay your hand on it, you can continue to paint without fear of smudging.

MAIN DESIGN

1 Trace the main details of the pattern as illustrated, then go over the tracing lines with fine outlines using either a brush pen or a liner loaded with Carbon Black. Once the outlines are completely dry, erase the tracing lines.

2 Referring to the colour illustration and using a No.4 round brush, paint the white as well as the light, medium and dark-toned areas. For all applications, use slow-drying medium to moisten your brush and to dilute the pigment. Brush-mix small amounts of pigment with medium until the tone approximately matches those that are illustrated. The sun and its aura uses Pale Gold. To save time, once the white and gold sun areas are painted, coat the whole of the remainder of the design with light Payne's Grey tone. These are the areas that look quite silvery on the illustration. Leave to dry.

3 Load the No.4 round brush with Pale Gold and paint over the initial light-toned Payne's Grey area of the forest canopy.

4 Then using a medium-toned Payne's Grey, paint all the medium-toned areas followed by all the dark-toned areas. Leave to dry.

5 Finally, with a dark-toned Payne's Grey, paint the dark-toned tree trunks and the deer. Allow to dry. Then add a further coat to the deer to make them stand out even more.

6 Load a No.3 round brush with Payne's Grey and paint the dark strokes of the forest canopy.

7 The contours in the immediate foreground need to be lightened now with Warm White. Dab the white on and rub it into place with your finger. For extra interest, add a series of side-loaded strokes on the far left contour using dilute Cobalt Blue.

8 Now add the hazy effect projecting downwards from the sun, around the deer and through the forest. It is most pronounced around the deer. Using a round flattened brush, dab on the Warm White paint moistened with slow-drying medium, first around the deer, and then on to other areas as illustrated. Use your finger or a mop to tease the paint out. I prefer the cruder effect of my finger! Use the dry-brush technique in places if you wish. Add more Warm White over the Pale Gold sun.

9 Reposition the pattern and trace the grass and floral positions. Paint the grass with strokes pulled from the base of the clumps. Use a variety of Payne's Grey tones as illustrated; use darker tones in the foreground and lighter ones as you retreat into the distance. For more variation, add Pale Gold to the Payne's Grey mixture in places.

10 Paint the flowers in the foreground with Cadmium Scarlet. For paler flowers, add a touch of Cadmium Scarlet to the White mixture. Integrate White and Carbon Black as illustrated in the flower centres. Use a stylus for the flowers and dot detail in the middle distance.

11 Reposition the pattern and trace the deer eyes and body lines. Using a 12mm (½ in) brush, highlight and shade with Warm White and Payne's Grey respectively. Add eye detail. Paint the hooves black.

12 Rule out the border and paint it black using a No.4 round brush.

FINISHING

Allow to dry for 24 hours. Erase the tracing lines, then apply two or three coats of water-based varnish, allowing each coat to dry before applying the next. Replace the handles on the chest.

COLOUR KEY

1 Silver
2 Payne's Grey
3 Warm White
4 Cadmium Scarlet
5 Carbon Black
6 Pale Gold
7 Cobalt Blue

DECORATIVE LANDSCAPE MIRROR

*W*HILE CLARICE CLIFF WAS DESIGNING AND DECORATING TEAPOTS IN ENGLAND, LUCIA MATHEWS WAS DECORATING FURNITURE IN AMERICA. WHAT THEY HAD IN COMMON WAS A FLAIR FOR DECORATIVE LANDSCAPES, WHICH AT THE TIME WAS HIGHLY ORIGINAL FOR PAINTED OBJECTS. CLARICE WAS INFLUENCED BY THE GEOMETRY AND COLOUR OF THE ART DECO PERIOD OF THE INTERWAR YEARS, WHEREAS LUCIA WAS MORE OF A TRADITIONALIST INFLUENCED BY THE ARTS AND CRAFTS MOVEMENT. THIS DESIGN IS AN ADAPTATION OF A DECORATIVE LANDSCAPE FROM AN APPLIED ART TEXTBOOK BY LOMOS , PUBLISHED IN 1933.

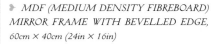

● materials ●

❧ *MDF (MEDIUM DENSITY FIBREBOARD) MIRROR FRAME WITH BEVELLED EDGE, 60cm × 40cm (24in × 16in)*

❧ BASE COAT
Vellum (Jo Sonja's background colour or similar substitute)

❧ FINISH
Acrylic satin finish spray

❧ PALETTE
Brown Earth, Warm White, Payne's Grey, Magenta, Storm Blue, Pthalo Green, Cadmium Yellow, Vermilion, Bronze, Teal Green

❧ BRUSHES
Large brush, 2.5cm (1in) flat, 12mm (½in) flat, No.4 round, No.3 round, liner

❧ OTHER SUPPLIES
Fine sandpaper, Jo Sonja's texture paste (or similar substitute), Lefranc & Bourgeois cracking varnish (or similar substitute), sponge, Burnt Umber artist's oil colour, soft cloth, surgical or methylated spirit (rubbing or denatured alcohol), acrylic satin spray finish, tracing paper, chalk pencil, slow-drying medium, eraser, black permanent pen, ruler, masking tape, coloured stone (optional), chisel, glue

BASE COAT

1   Using a large brush, apply two or three coats of Vellum background paint over the frame, including the bevel. Sand gently between coats when dry.

2   Apply two or three coats of texture paste around the bevel, allowing each coat to dry before sanding. This prevents the sanded surface forming 'peach fuzz'.

3   Using a 2.5cm (1in) flat brush, apply one coat of cracking varnish on the flat part of the frame. Avoid touching it until it is absolutely dry, or it will mark. You can use a hair dryer to speed up the drying process. Apply a second coat of varnish, and allow it to dry. The cracks will not be obvious at this stage.

4   Dab a small piece of sponge into Burnt Umber

Painting Style

The painting style of this project is bold, using transparent washes as its basis. The lining is kept to a minimum.
Shading is blended rather than applied by the sideloading method

artist's oil colour and dust it over the frame very lightly. Don't be tempted to use acrylic Burnt Umber as, being water-based, it will lift off the crackle.

5   Douse a soft cloth with surgical or methylated spirit (rubbing or denatured alcohol) and wipe this over the surface (see page 22). Wipe the bevel too, to give it a slightly 'dirty' film for an aged look.

6   Allow to dry, then spray with acrylic satin spray finish. Do not substitute a water-based varnish.

DESIGN

1   Position the pattern on the mirror frame and trace on the border.

2   Apply two coats of Brown Earth in the border using a No.4 round brush. Allow to dry.

3   Using a No.4 round brush, apply two or three coats of Warm White over the whole inside area. Allow to dry.

4   Trace on the contours of the skyline only. Saturate a 12mm (½ in) flat brush with slow-drying medium, then pick up a touch of Payne's Grey and blend. On the same brush, pick up a tiny amount of Magenta and blend, then pick up more if you need to. A light bright mauve is the colour you are aiming for.

5   Apply this colour to the sky area as well as allowing it to spill over the contours of the skyline. Be brave, you don't need to be precise! Dry with a hair dryer.

6   Clean the brush, then saturate with slow-drying medium. Now pick up a small amount of Storm Blue and apply it to the entire ground area. Allow to dry. Apply a second coat over the contour on the left and leave to dry.

7   Clean the brush, saturate with slow-drying medium, then pick up a tint of Pthalo Green and lightly brush this over the contoured area on the right. Look closely at the first illustration and you will see a faint 'V' swathe where the tint has been blended in. Leave to dry.

8   Trace on the sinking sun. Erase the trace marks to a faint line. Using a No.4 round brush, apply one light coat of Cadmium Yellow, then a light coat of Vermilion, and finally a light coat of Bronze on the sun. Moisten the brush each time with slow-drying medium to achieve a transparent effect.

9   Trace on the trees. Moisten a No.3 round brush with slow-drying medium and blend with Brown Earth. Paint the tree trunks from top to bottom, allowing the strokes to tail off unevenly at their bases. Blend a second coat on the tree trunks to create a shadowed effect on the right of each one.

10   Trace on the flowers. Use the tip of a No.3 round brush to dab on the background flowers with Warm White. Flatten the same brush, load with slow-drying medium and Warm White and paint the rest of the flowers. Apply a second coat of Warm White to accentuate some of the flowers, especially

those in the foreground. Don't clean the brush.

11 Using the same brush, pick up a touch of Payne's Grey, blend to make a darker shade, and just lightly touch it into each flower centre.

12 Moisten a liner with slow-drying medium, roll it into a mixture of Warm White and Payne's Grey and paint the faint suggestion of stems leading from the central dab just applied. Remember that these flowers are facing towards the last light of the sun, so you will be painting an impression of their backs. Leave to dry.

13 Trace on the vegetation in the foreground. Using a No.4 round brush moistened with slow-drying medium, pick up a tiny amount of Teal Green and lightly wash it into the foreground. Then, using a liner rolled in the Warm White and Payne's Grey mixture, lightly suggest the foreground outlines. Leave to dry.

14 Moisten a liner with slow-drying medium and mix Brown Earth and Payne's Grey. Roll the brush into a point and then outline the trees, and, very lightly, a few flowers. Leave to dry.

15 Using a black permanent pen and ruler, outline the outside border. I did not erase my tracing lines because I think they add to the effect, but you can decide for yourself!

FINISHING

1 Spray the finished design with two or three coats of acrylic satin finish spray, allowing it to dry between coats.

2 If liked, paint some masking tape with Brown Earth, cut it into small squares and stick these on to the design. This is a good way to test the finished effect, painting the squares on afterwards if it is to your taste!

OPTIONAL STONE INSET

I borrowed the following idea from artists of the Arts and Crafts and Art Nouveau periods. They liked to inset semi-precious stones into some of their work.

1 Position the stone, then use a chalk pencil to draw an outline round it.

2 Using a chisel, begin hollowing out a well, starting in the centre and working outwards, stopping within 6–12mm (¼–½ in) of your outline.

3 From here, you will need to judge the contours of your stone and chisel out the remainder accordingly until it sits to your satisfaction.

4 Affix the stone in place with suitable glue.

COLOUR KEY
1 Brown Earth
2 Payne's Grey
3 Vermilion
4 Teal Green
5 Magenta
6 Cadmium Yellow
7 Warm White
8 Storm Blue
9 Pthalo Green
10 Bronze

GEORGIA O'KEEFE REVELRY

GEORGIA O'KEEFE (1887–1986) WAS ONE OF AMERICA'S BEST-LOVED FINE ARTISTS. FOR HER, THE CLOSE-UP VIEW DEEP INTO THE BOWELS OF THE BLOOM WAS A FAVOURITE THEME AND THE SMOOTHNESS OF HER BLENDED TECHNIQUE WAS ONE OF THE CHIEF CHARACTERISTICS OF HER PAINTING STYLE. THIS BOX WAS PAINTED AS A CELEBRATION OF HER UNIQUE WORK.

Painting Style

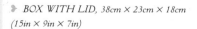

In this project, layering and blending techniques are combined to create a vibrant build-up of translucent colour using a contemporary close-up image

---

• materials •

❧ **BOX WITH LID,** *38cm × 23cm × 18cm (15in × 9in × 7in)*

❧ **BASE COAT**
Teal Green, Warm White

❧ **FINISH**
Water-based varnish

❧ **PALETTE**
Warm White, Payne's Grey, Aqua, Pthalo Green, Cadmium Yellow, Brilliant Green, Nimbus Grey, Moss Green, Teal Green, Burnt Umber, Pale Gold, Carbon Black

❧ **BRUSHES**
Large brush, No.4 round, No.3 mop, No.3 round, 6mm (¼ in) flat, liner, No.8 round

❧ **OTHER SUPPLIES**
Fine sandpaper, tracing paper, graphite paper, chalk pencil, ruler, slow-drying medium, paper towel, black permanent pen, eraser

BASE COAT

1 Mix together Teal Green and Warm White in equal proportions. Using a large brush, apply three coats of this colour on the box, sanding lightly between each coat when dry.

2 Trace on the box the perimeter of the rectangle, using a chalk pencil and ruler. Then apply two coats of Warm White inside the rectangle, allowing the first coat to dry before applying the second.

3 Reposition the pattern and trace on the perimeter of the inner rectangle using a ruler, and then trace the main outlines of the pattern.

DESIGN

Use all pigments sparingly and mix them with generous quantities of slow-drying medium. Use a hair dryer to dry each application.

1 Apply Payne's Grey mixture on to the background areas using a No.4 round brush. Blot the paint with a paper towel after each application. Apply two or three coats, if necessary, to match the colour illustration.

2 Apply Aqua mixture on to the leaves and calyx. Leave to dry.

3 Overpaint the leaves and calyx with Pthalo Green mixture. Allow to dry.

4 Overpaint the leaves and calyx again with Cadmium Yellow mixture. Leave to dry.

5 Apply two coats of Warm White mixture on to the petals. Begin the strokes on the outer edge and tail them off at the centre. Leave to dry. Reposition the pattern and trace on the petal divisions, leaf veins and outer central halo.

6 Load a No.4 round brush with Brilliant Green and dab a small amount into the centre of the flower as illustrated (1). Then, using a No.3 mop brush, tease the paint out into the central area to the periphery of the halo (2).

7 Sideload Nimbus Grey and paint first the main petal divisions, then the subdivisions. Leave to dry. Sideload with a touch of Payne's Grey and overpaint the main petal divisions.

8 Load a No.4 round brush with Cadmium Yellow mixture and dab a small amount into the centre and around the halo periphery (2), then use the mop to tease it out as shown (3).

9 Dab small amounts of Payne's Grey mixture on to the petals (3), then use a mop to tease it out into the light shaded areas (4).

10 Load a No.3 round brush with Cadmium Yellow and Moss Green mixture in the ratio of 2:1, and then paint the leaf veins.

11 Sideload a 6mm (¼ in) flat brush with Teal Green and lightly shade around the leaf veins and on the calyx. Leave to dry. Overpaint with Cadmium Yellow mixture to dampen the sharpness of the veins. Allow to dry.

12 Dab Payne's Grey mixture on to the left leaf and tease it out to create a shaded area as illustrated. Dab Payne's Grey around the petal edges, then tease it out to bring the flowerhead into greater prominence.

13 Dab a small amount of Burnt Umber mixture into the flower centre (4) and tease it out. Leave to dry. Reposition the pattern and trace the details of the flower centre.

14 Roll a liner in Payne's Grey mixture and outline the details. Leave to dry.

15 Sideload a 6mm (¼ in) flat brush with Moss Green and apply as illustrated (5).

FINISHING

1 Using a ruler and permanent pen, apply the black border outlines. Then apply the Pale Gold outlines using a liner. Paint a series of diagonal Carbon Black lines on top of the white border area using a liner.

2 Flatten a No.8 round brush, load it with Pale Gold mixture and paint round the bevelled edge of the box.

3 Add Pale Gold rectangle boxes on the upright surfaces.

4 Allow to dry for 24 hours, then erase any tracing lines, and finally apply two or three coats of water-based varnish, allowing each coat to dry before applying the next.

COLOUR KEY

1 Payne's Grey
2 Aqua
3 Brilliant Green
4 Pthalo Blue
5 Warm White
6 Moss Green
7 Cadmium Yellow
8 Nimbus Grey
9 Burnt Umber
10 Teal Green
11 Pale Gold
12 Carbon Black

1

2

3

4

11   1   2   3   4   5   12

6   7   8   9   10

5

Airmail Nasturtiums

Developing a design to suit an object is a stimulating process. I wanted a novel idea that everyone would recognize, and an airmail envelope seemed perfect! This bottle rack proved to be eminently suitable for my adaptation. The stringent discipline of stamp design – the creation of a strong, clear visual image within the confines of such a small space – was challenging. The airmail candy stripes, however, slotted naturally on to the tapered edging, as did the stamp and sticker on to the front piece.

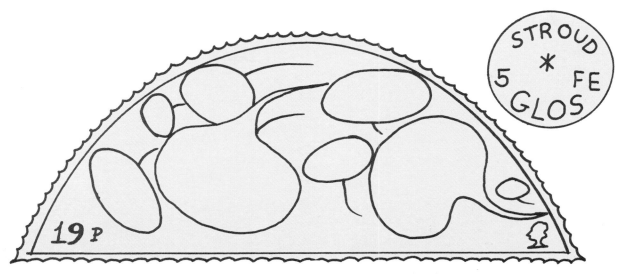

Painting Style

This is very much a contemporary approach for using strokework. The stroke shapes are not perfect, but used suggestively. Deliberate avoidance of overworking the paint is the aim as flat, dry brush strokes are combined with wet dollop strokes

• m a t e r i a l s •

▶ *CONDIMENT BOTTLE RACK*
23cm × 9cm × 27cm (9in × 3½in × 10½in)

▶ BASE COAT
Soft White (Jo Sonja's background colour or similar substitute)

▶ FINISH
Water-based varnish

▶ PALETTE
Colony Blue, French Blue, Vermilion, Carbon Black, Warm White, Cadmium

Scarlet, Cadmium Yellow, Green Oxide, Moss Green, Rich Gold, Fawn

▶ BRUSHES
Large brush, No.8 round, liner, 6mm (¼ in) flat, 3mm (⅛ in) flat, No.4 round

▶ OTHER SUPPLIES
Brown paper bag, tracing paper, graphite paper, chalk pencil, paper towel, slow-drying medium, eraser

BASE COAT

1   Using a large brush, apply three coats of Soft White background paint over the bottle rack, sanding between coats when dry with a brown paper bag.

2   Brush-mix equal proportions of Colony Blue and French Blue. Dilute this mixture to a watery

consistency and, using a No.8 round brush, paint the bevelled edge at the bottom of the rack and all other edges except those reserved for airmail stripes. Load a liner with Vermilion and apply this alongside the blue.

3   Transfer the design outlines on to the bottle rack (see page 24).

AIRMAIL STRIPES AND STICKER

1   Load a 6mm (¼in) flat brush with equal proportions of Colony Blue and French Blue and paint the diagonal blue stripes.

2   Load the same brush with Vermilion and paint the red stripes.

3   Load a 3mm (⅛in) flat brush with blue mix and paint the long sticker stripe; then paint the red stripe. Add the red lettering using the same brush.

DATE STAMP

1   Load a liner with Carbon Black and paint the circle and lettering. Allow to dry.

2   Blend a tiny amount of Warm White into a 6mm (¼in) flat brush. Dilute with a little water and blend again. Blot on a paper towel, then brush it over the date stamp, softening the black and creating a realistic, slightly smudged look.

SEMI-CIRCLE STAMP

LEFT FLOWER

1   Paint three dry-brushed flat strokes as illustrated using a 6mm (¼in) flat brush and Cadmium Scarlet paint.

2   Make the fourth stroke a dry-brushed comma stroke, to suggest the tail.

3   Make the fifth stroke another shorter comma stroke, again dry-brushed.

RIGHT FLOWER

1   Using a 6mm (¼in) flat brush, paint the first two dry-brush strokes as illustrated.

2   Make the third stroke a comma; make the fourth another comma placed next to the first stroke; make the fifth stroke sit on top of the third.

3   Load a liner with Cadmium Yellow and suggest the central stamens with comma strokes.

LEAVES

1   Using a No.8 round brush loaded with Green Oxide, paint six dollop strokes as illustrated: three

with tails going up and three with tails going down. If the paint takes on a crackled look as you lift the brush, all well and good – work with the impression you get. Do not wash the brush out.

2   Pick up some Moss Green and blend, then on top of the three dollops on the left, place a second dollop.

3   Using a No.4 round brush, add Moss Green strokes at the bottom of the three right-hand strokes made earlier.

4   Load a liner with Warm White, and paint a suggestion of veins as illustrated.

5   Roll the liner in undermixed Moss Green and Green Oxide, then paint the stems.

DETAILS

1   Load a liner with Rich Gold and paint the monarch's head.

2   Load a liner with Vermilion and paint a faint outline of a stamp.

3   Load a liner with Carbon Black and paint a jagged stamp outline.

4   Moisten a 6mm (¼in) flat brush with slow-drying medium and sideload with Fawn, then run it around the stamp edge to create the shadow.

FINISHING

Allow to dry for 24 hours, then erase all tracing lines. Apply three coats of water-based varnish, allowing to dry and sanding with a brown paper bag between coats.

COLOUR KEY

1 *Cadmium Scarlet*	7 *Carbon Black*
2 *Vermilion*	8 *Colony Blue*
3 *Fawn*	9 *French Blue*
4 *Green Oxide*	10 *Cadmium Yellow*
5 *Moss Green*	11 *Rich Gold*
6 *Warm White*	

19 P

VIA AIR MAIL

STROUD
*
5 FE
GLOS

1950s *MAGAZINE RACK*

*A*FTER WORLD WAR I, THE BLOOMSBURY SET OF LONDON WERE THE FIRST TO UPSET THE STATUS QUO OF THE ART COMMUNITY. 'VULGAR' EXUBERANT COLOUR AND ABANDONMENT OF REALISTIC DRAUGHTSMANSHIP EXPRESSED THE NEW PERSONAL AND ARTISTIC FREEDOM. THIS TREND WAS TO CONTINUE WITH POST-WAR MODERNISM AFTER WORLD WAR II WITH ITS OWN PECULIAR FEATURES. DECORATIVE DESIGN WAS NO LESS INFLUENCED BY THESE TRENDS. A DOMINANT MOTIF WAS THE ORGANIC AMOEBA-LIKE BLOB COMBINED WITH DESIGNS OF MINIMAL STYLING, BOTH OF WHICH COMPRISE THIS RATHER DARING '50S PIECE.

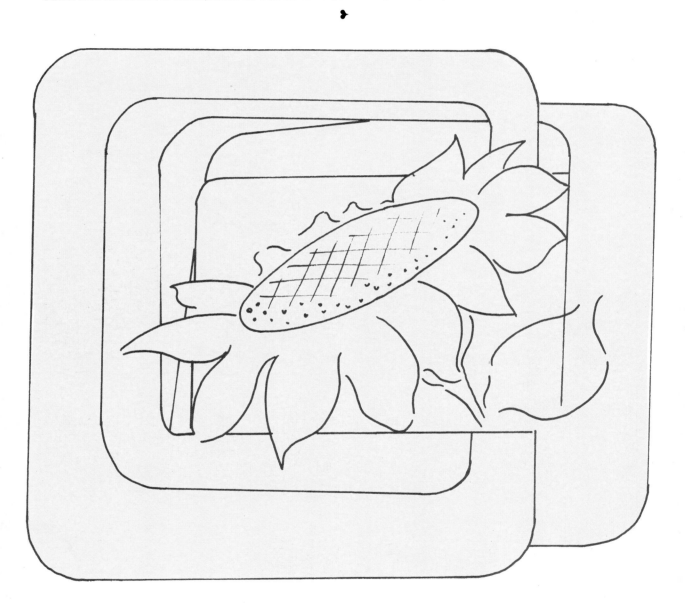

Painting Style

The dominant look of this piece suggests the hand of bold painting, but it also includes strokework: leaf strokes for the petals and a run-on flat stroke winding from the outer section into the centre of the blobs. The movement of the brush strokes makes a strong and unusual statement

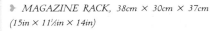

● m a t e r i a l s ●

❧ *MAGAZINE RACK, 38cm × 30cm × 37cm (15in × 11½in × 14in)*

❧ BASE COAT
White (Jo Sonja's background colour or similar substitute)

❧ FINISH
Water-based varnish

❧ PALETTE
Aqua, Ultramarine Blue, Warm White, Vermilion, Napthol Red Light, Burgundy, Rose Pink, Turners Yellow, Cadmium Yellow, Carbon Black

❧ BRUSHES
Large brush, 12mm (½in) flat, No.4 round, 6mm (¼in) flat, liner

❧ OTHER SUPPLIES
Brown paper bag, tracing paper, graphite paper, chalk pencil, ruler, slow-drying medium, stylus, eraser

BASE COAT

1   Using a large brush, apply three coats of White background paint on to the magazine rack, sanding between each coat with a brown paper bag when dry. With the same brush, apply two or three coats of Aqua to the inside surfaces and the edging. Leave to dry.

2   Paint random blobs, some in Ultramarine Blue and others in Aqua on to the white background. Vary the size and shapes of the blobs, and make squares or oblongs. Overlap some of the blobs in varying degrees. For each blob, load enough paint on to a 12mm (½in) flat brush to complete the run-on stroke. Allow to dry.

GEOMETRIC AND FLORAL MOTIF

1   Position the pattern over the painted background, slightly off-centre, then trace the outside edge of the pattern (see page 24). Apply three coats of Warm White over the transferred pattern. Reposition the pattern and trace everything except the stem and leaf. Use a ruler for the straight edges.

2   Load a No.4 round brush with Aqua and apply two coats to the inner oblong. When applying the second coat, allow some of the paint to overlap the petal edges. Using the same brush, paint two coats of Warm White with a touch of Vermilion on to the next shape. Then paint two coats of Napthol Red Light mixed with Burgundy in the ratio of 2:1 on to the next shape. Moisten the same brush with slow-drying medium, then load it with Rose Pink and apply two coats to the outermost oblong. (The random blobs are intended to show through the motif in varying degrees.)

3   Load a 6mm (¼in) flat brush with undermixed Turners Yellow and Cadmium Yellow. Use a leaf stroke to paint the petals, which need not follow the tracing lines precisely.

4   Reapply the pattern and trace the petals, the central portion of the flower and the stem and leaf.

5   Using a liner, line the petals with loose free movements in Carbon Black. Then outline the stem and leaf.

6   Load a No.4 round brush with Carbon Black and paint the centre of the sunflower. Using a stylus, apply dots in the centre in Turners Yellow and Warm White.

7   Using a liner, apply cross-hatching to the centre and add white outlines along the black leaf outline.

FINISHING

Allow to dry for 24 hours, then erase the tracing lines. Finally, apply two or three coats of water-based varnish, allowing each coat to dry before applying the next one.

COLOUR KEY

1	*Cobalt Blue*	*6*	*Burgundy*
2	*Aqua*	*7*	*Rose Pink*
3	*Warm White*	*8*	*Carbon Black*
4	*Vermilion*	*9*	*Cadmium Yellow*
5	*Napthol Red Light*	*10*	*Turners Yellow*

CONTEMPORARY ANEMONES

THIS PROJECT INTRODUCES A FRESH LOOK FOR COLOURFUL AND BOLD CONTEMPORARY LIVING. THIS IS A NEW DEPARTURE FOR AN ART FORM WHICH TENDS TO ERR ON THE CONSERVATIVE SIDE. MOREOVER, IT DEMONSTRATES THAT THE SCOPE OF THIS ART FORM IS AS EXPANSIVE AS THAT OF ITS FINE ART COUNTERPART. DESPITE ITS CONTEMPORARY LOOK, THIS DESIGN UTILIZES MANY OF THE DECORATIVE PAINTER'S BASIC TECHNIQUES, WHILE ALSO INTRODUCING ONE OR TWO FROM THE FINE ART DISCIPLINE.

Painting Style

The project uses the bold techniques of line, wash and sideloading. Even the white lines of the tracing are not rubbed out so that they become a part of the overall effect. The paint is used quite wet, and simply applied to the relevant spaces without thinking about strokes. The look starts to come together when the black lines are added. Don't try to follow the traced lines religiously. A loose scribbled effect is better

● m a t e r i a l s ●

❧ *TRAY, 50cm × 38cm (20in × 15½in)*

❧ BASE COAT
Azure (Jo Sonja's background colour or similar substitute)

❧ FINISH
Water-based varnish

❧ PALETTE
Aqua, Warm White, Pthalo Blue, Prussian Blue, Dioxin Purple, Napthol Red Light, Transparent Magenta, Cobalt Blue, Moss Green, Green Oxide,

Carbon Black, Payne's Grey, Teal Green, Cadmium Yellow

❧ BRUSHES
Large brush, old brush, No.4 round brush, liner, 12mm (½in) flat, 6mm (¼in) flat

❧ OTHER SUPPLIES
Tracing paper, white chalk pencil, graphite paper, masking fluid, 4 jar lids or small receptacles, brush pen (see page 54 – optional), masking tape, clear glazing medium, rubber comb, brown paper bag

BASE COAT

1 Using a large brush, paint the tray with three coats of Azure background colour, allowing each coat to dry before applying the next.

2 Transfer the outer edge of the main design rectangle on to the tray (see page 24). Paint three coats of the Warm White into the rectangle.

3 Transfer the floral pattern outlines on to the tray. Select an old brush, one that you won't mind throwing out. Shake the masking fluid well. Dip your brush into it and begin filling in the pattern on the tray. Don't worry if the fluid runs over the lines a bit. Allow it to dry; as it dries, the colour changes from creamy to bright yellow. Masking fluid allows you to paint over the masked areas without spoiling what is underneath.

4 Take four jar lids. Squeeze a tiny amount of Aqua, Pthalo Blue, Prussian Blue and Dioxin Purple into the lids. Dilute each colour so that it becomes a watery solution. With a wide brush (3–4cm/ 1¼–1½ in), apply a strip of Aqua on the far left of the tray, then when that has dried brush on a strip of Pthalo Blue, followed by Prussian Blue, followed by Dioxin Purple. There is no need to adhere to the exact widths and colours of the strips shown. Experiment on a piece of paper first. The strips can overlap. Dry-brush some Prussian Blue and Dioxin Purple on to the right hand strip so that they mingle interestingly with the washes, darkening as you move to the right. Finally, wash some paint in a diagonal sweep on the left. Allow all the paint to dry.

5 Remove the masking fluid by rubbing over it with your fingers to expose the white background.

FLOWERS

1 Using a No.4 brush, base in all the flowers and stems as illustrated using Napthol Red Light, Transparent Magenta and Cobalt Blue mixed with a little Dioxin Purple. Use Moss Green for the lighter stems and Green Oxide for the darker ones. Mix the paint quite thinly so that it goes on as water-colour. Push the paint around in each designated area rather than painting precise tidy strokes. This will add character. Allow to dry.

2 Reposition the pattern and, using white graphite paper, trace over the design. If it is slightly off kilter, it will add to the effect!

3 Paint in the flower centres with Warm White. With a brush pen (or a liner and Carbon Black, if you prefer), add the outlines. Be fluid and loose rather than tightly precise. Dab in the black centres. Don't erase any of the white tracing lines.

4 Sideload shadows on to the petals using a darker tone of each flower colour, together with a touch of Payne's Grey, and a 6mm (¼ in) flat brush.

5 Shade between the stems using a combination of Teal Green and Prussian Blue using the sideload method. Sideload Pthalo Blue halos around some of the flower petals as illustrated. Sideload Warm White halos around the buds and the upper right-hand blue flower.

6 Using a 12mm (½ in) flat brush, wash some Cadmium Yellow into the design periphery in places as shown. Add diminishing Warm White dots, then, when completely dry, wash them over with Pthalo Blue.

7 Outline the rectangle in black with a brush pen or a liner.

BORDER

1 Measure out the combed border (5cm/2in) and stick masking tape around its inside edge. Mix a dab of Payne's Grey with approximately 30ml (2 tablespoons) of clear glazing medium in a jar lid. Using a wide brush, apply it generously into the demarcated area.

2 Run a rubber comb along the perimeter of the tray. Draw it steadily from corner to corner, beginning and ending on each corner at a 45-degree angle.

3 When dry, use a white chalk pencil to outline the outside and inside edge of the combed border as well as the central panel for a soft effect.

FINISHING

Allow the paint to dry for 24 hours. Apply two or three coats of water-based varnish over the tray, allowing each coat to dry and then sanding with a paper bag, before applying the next coat.

LIST OF SUPPLIERS

BRUSH DISTRIBUTORS
USA
Loew Cornell Brushes
563 Chestnut Avenue
Teaneck
NJ 07666–2490

CANADA
Maureen McNaughton
RRT 2
Belwood
ON NOB1JO

PAINT DISTRIBUTORS
(Water-based paints and related
products for the decorative art
market)

DecoArt Products
UK
Corner House Crafts
4 Park Lane
Shaftesbury
Dorset SP7 8JR

USA
DecoArt
PO Box 386
Stanford
KY 40484

Delta Ceramcoat Products
UK
George Weil & Son Ltd
The Warehouse
Reading Circle Road
Redhill
Surrey RH1 1HG

Liquitext products
UK
Binney & Smith (Europe) Ltd
Amphill Road
Bedford MK42 9RS

USA
Binney & Smith Inc
1100 Church Lane
PO Box 431
Easton
PA 18044–0431

CANADA
Binney & Smith (Canada) Ltd
Toronto Sales & Distribution Office
40 East Pearce Street
Richmond Hill
Ontario L4B 1B7

AUSTRALIA
Binney & Smith (Australia) Ltd
599 Blackburn Road
Clayton North 3168
PO Box 684
Glen Waverly 3150
Victoria

Jo Sonja products
UK
Tomas Seth & Co
Holly House
Castle Hill
Hartley
Kent DA3 7BH

USA
Chroma Acrylics Inc
205 Bucky Drive
Lititz
PA 17543

AUSTRALIA & JAPAN
Chroma Acrylics (NSW) Pty Ltd
PO Box 3B
Mt Kuring-Gai
NSW 2080

SUNDRY ITEMS
(Unfinished wooden objects, tinware,
ceramics, brushes, paints, sealer,
medium, books and publications)

Cottage Folk Art
7 Church Street
Beaminster
Dorset DT8 3BA

Dee's School of Folk and
    Decorative Art
The Studio
7 Glenville Road
Kingston-upon-Thames
Surrey KT2 6DD

Goodhands Decorative Folk
    Art Studio
1 Bentley Close
Horndean
Waterlooville
Hampshire PO8 9HH

Special Effects
    Decorative Arts Studio
251 Archway Road
Highgate
London N6 5EU

Tahira's School of Decorative
    Painting
5A Royal Crescent
London W11 4SL

Trip the Daisey
Idstone
Swindon
Wiltshire SN6 8LL

OTHER USEFUL ADDRESSES
UK
British Association of Decorative &
    Folk Arts
1 Bentley Close
Horndean
Waterlooville
Hampshire PO8 9HH

USA
Artist's Journal
PO Box 9080
Eureka
CA 95501
Decorative art journal published
quarterly by Jo Sonja Inc.

The Decorative Painter
PO Box 808
Newton
KS 67114
Magazine published bi-monthly by
the Society of Decorative Painters.

National Society of Tole &
    Decorative Painters
393 North McLean Blvd
Witchita
KS 67203–5968

BIBLIOGRAPHY

Anscombe, Isabelle, *Arts & Crafts Style* (Phaidon Press 1991)

Atterbury, Paul, *The History of Porcelain* (Orbis Publishing Ltd 1982)

Battersby, Martin, *The Decorative Twenties* (The Herbert Press 1988)

Bridgewater, Alan and Gill, *Traditional and Folk Designs* (Search Press 1990)

Christie, Archibald, *Pattern Design – An Introduction to the Study of Formal Ornament* (Dover Publications 1969)

Clifton-Mogg, Caroline, *The Neo-Classical Sourcebook* (Cassell 1991)

Crump, Derek, *The Complete Guide to Wood Finishes* (HarperCollins 1992)

de Dampierre, Florence, *The Best of Painted Furniture* (Weidenfeld & Nicolson 1987)

The Designs of William de Morgan (Dennis & Wiltshire 1989)

Dresdner, Michael, *The Woodfinishing Book* (The Taunton Press 1992)

Garner, Philippe, *The Contemporary Decorative Arts* (Phaidon Press 1980)

Graburn, Nelson H. H., *Ethnic and Tourist Arts – Cultural Expressions from the Fourth World* (University of California Press 1979)

Hardy, William, *A Guide to Art Nouveau Style* (Magna Books 1992)

Jones, Owen, *The Grammar of Ornament* (Studio Editions 1986)

Klein, Dan, and Bishop, Margaret, *Decorative Art 1880–1980* (Phaidon Press 1986)

Licthen, Frances, *Folk Art Motifs of Pennsylvania* (Dover Publications 1954)

Miller, Judith and Martin, *Period Finishes and Effects* (Mitchell Beazley 1992)

Morgan, Sarah, *Art Deco* (Bison Books 1990)

Parry, Linda, *William Morris and the Arts & Crafts Movement – A Source Book* (Portland House 1989)

Peesch, Reinhard, *The Ornament in European Folk Art* (Alpine Fine Arts Collection 1983)

Ridges, Bob, *The Decoy Duck from Folk Art to Fine Art* (Dragon's World 1988)

Ritz, Gisland, *The Art of Painted Furniture* (Von Nostrand Reinhold Company 1971)

Robertson, Pamela, *Charles Rennie Mackintosh* (Pavilion Books 1995)

Rust, Graham, *The Painted House* (Cassell 1988), *Decorative Designs* (Cassell 1996)

Tymms, W. R., *The Art of Illuminating* (Studio Editions 1987)

Wilson, Althea, *Paint Works* (Century Hutchinson Ltd 1988)

INDEX